the John F. Kennedy handbook

Gareth Jenkins

MQP

MQ Publications Ltd

JFK

His father's son

John F. Kennedy came from a boisterous, energetic, Boston Irish family which reveled in the rough world of politics — both his grandfathers were politicians. His parents were already rich and would soon head one of the wealthiest families in the United States, although the sources of that money were hardly visible.

Young Jack was sickly from birth, and throughout his life he suffered from a bewildering array of ailments, many of which remained mysterious. His youth was punctuated with long spells in bed, at home, at boarding school, and in expensive clinics. Showered with affection by an over-bearing father, and denied it by an emotionally cold mother, he grew up craving love and warmth. He was the most gregarious of boys, and yet always apart.

Given his frail health, most parents would have encouraged a son like Jack to pursue a career that would not place too many demands on him. But the Kennedy ethic required that all the children had to strive to be first, both on the sports field and in the public world.

The highest expectations were for the first born, Joseph Jr. But he died young, and Jack was compelled to take his place, as were his younger brothers Robert and Edward in their turn. The Kennedys were nothing if not a team, imbued with fierce loyalty. Their goal was to escape the stigma attaching to their Irish Catholic origins and win their place at the top in American public life.

Previous page: **News conference, State Department, November 20, 1962**
Kennedy was the first president to give live television press conferences.

Fate deals some surprising hands. All the personal accounts of friends, all the biographies, paint a picture of the young Jack Kennedy struggling to be free, scorning social constraints and conformity, reckless in his pursuit of women, leaving hostages to fortune at every turn. Yet always at his back was his domineering father, Joseph Sr., keeping Jack's anarchic free spirit in check, clearing up his mess, and pointing him from an early age in the direction of the presidency. The only one of the family who really broke free of the father was Jack's favorite sister Kathleen, who did it by marrying into the British Protestant aristocracy.

Many have argued that as he matured, Jack developed his own ideas and became his own man. It is true he left behind, or learned to hide, some of his father's more extreme reactionary ideas, such as Joe Sr.'s crude anti-semitism and his admiration for Hitler. He also occasionally went against paternal advice, notably as a senator when he and his brother Bobby both worked on a committee to root out corruption and mob influence in the labor unions.

 But it was Joe Sr. who financed all Jack's political campaigns, and on a scale unheard of in America at the time. And it was Joe who controlled strategy, called in favors, bribed officials, and, most crucially of all, ensured the support of the media. Even during Jack's first year in the White House, until Joe was struck down by a stroke, there was a private telephone line in a room off the Oval Office from which Jack would take advice from his father.

Joe was the genius who pushed his sons forward. A man of acute intelligence and unhindered by ethical concerns, after making his millions he developed ambitions to become president. President Roosevelt appointed him ambassador to London, but then he threw away his chances by trying to make a secret deal with Hitler to keep

America out of the war. For this he earned the undying hatred of Roosevelt and Winston Churchill. From then on he devoted himself entirely to manipulating his sons' careers from the shadows.

Joe was not simply a lone maverick. His political views reflected the dominant view of the U.S. State Department in the twenties and thirties that Hitler was the best bulwark against Soviet Russia. As Hitler increasingly threatened U.S. interests, Roosevelt led America towards war with Germany in alliance with Britain.

As a young man Jack Kennedy's views evolved along with the new foreign policy consensus. His father may not have shared these views, but he supported his son and did everything to push forward his career. Nevertheless, there was nothing liberal about Kennedy's politics before he made his run for the presidency. As a senator he supported Senator McCarthy's anti-communist witch hunt, and nearly failed to win the support of Eleanor Roosevelt's wing of the Democratic Party as a result. Of all the senators, Kennedy was among the most ardent champions of the Cold War.

One of the great paradoxes was that Kennedy's youthful appeal, his animal spirits, and evident lust for life, were daily undermined by his chronic ill health. He scarcely knew a day without severe pain, yet even those closest to him were often unaware of the agony he suffered. On several occasions he came very close to death. Yet his family somehow managed to keep his illnesses carefully concealed from public gaze.

Medical evidence has slowly filtered out suggesting that if he had not been assassinated, Kennedy might not have survived a second term in office. His spinal column was disintegrating from years of cortisone injections, and his Addison's disease could have ended his life at any moment. His pain was kept at bay with daily injections of a potent cocktail of drugs that included methedrine.

Cuba was the scarlet thread that ran right through Kennedy's presidency. It was on the issue of support for a Cuban émigré invasion of the island that Kennedy trapped Richard Nixon in his campaign for the presidency. Once in the White House, it was the disastrous CIA invasion of Cuba at the Bay of Pigs that dealt Kennedy his first and greatest defeat, within three months of taking office. His obsession with exacting revenge—which he shared with most of the U.S. political elite—led him to initiate a campaign of sabotage against Cuba, numerous attempts to assassinate Castro, and plans for a second invasion, this time using U.S. troops. It was this aggression that led to Cuba accepting nuclear missiles from the Russians, and the missile crisis of October 1962. Before Kennedy could save the world, he brought it closer to destruction than any time before or since.

His Cold War zeal led him into initiating full-scale counter-insurgency in South Vietnam. He conducted back channel diplomacy with the Russians without informing his advisers, and he presided over secret plans to assassinate foreign leaders.

Kennedy was a contradictory figure. He was considered a political lightweight until he made it to the presidency and was habitually cautious. Yet he demonstrated nerves of steel during the missile crisis. Many people who worked with him have attested to his great magnetism and genuine charm. He was the first celebrity politician of the television age, the patrician with the common touch whom the American public felt they knew. And yet for all his apparent accessibility, forty years on they are still little closer to knowing Kennedy the politician behind the amiable mask.

Note: All quotations are from John F. Kennedy, unless otherwise indicated.

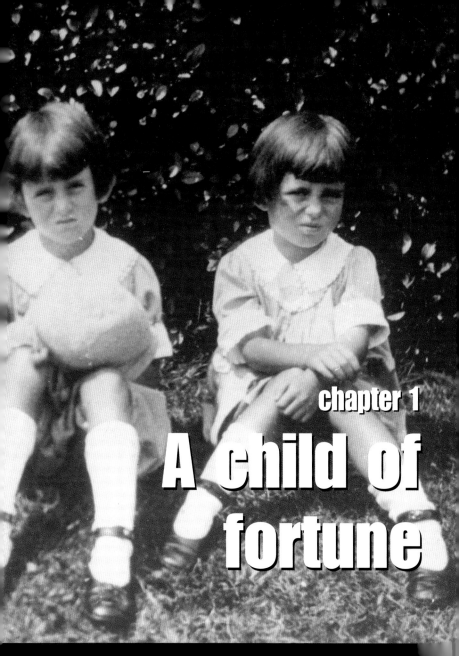

chapter 1

A child of fortune

The making of a dynasty

John Fitzgerald Kennedy was born into a prosperous Boston family on May 29, 1917. His parents, Joseph Patrick and Rose, had married in 1914 and already had a son, Joe Jr., who was nearly two years old. Seven more children were to follow over the next fifteen years. The family, on both sides, had come a long way in half a century, since Jack's great-grandparents had fled Ireland following the potato famines of the 1840s. His paternal grandfather, Patrick Joseph Kennedy, began work as a stevedore, then built a saloon and whiskey import business. He went into politics and served for five years in the Massachusetts Lower House, followed by six years in the state Senate. In his later years he was a power broker in Massachusetts politics.

Jack was named for his maternal grandfather, John F. Fitzgerald. Widely known as Honey Fitz for his easy manner, he went even further as a politician. Educated at one of Boston's leading high schools, he went on to Harvard Medical School but abandoned medicine for politics. He was elected to the state Senate in 1892 at the age of twenty-nine, and two years later won Boston's Ninth District seat in Congress—one of only three Catholic Representatives at the time. He was elected Mayor of Boston in 1905, but two years later lost his re-election bid under suspicion of corruption. Honey Fitz got back for a second term in 1910, but his attempt to win a third term was wrecked in 1913 when his opponent smeared him publicly for his relationship with a woman in New York, known to all by her nickname, "Toodles."

Previous page: **Jack aged eight, with his sisters Rosemary, Kathleen, and Eunice, 1925**

Jack's father, Joe Sr., set his mind on business success at an early age. At high school he not only excelled at athletics but, aged fifteen, organized his own baseball team, collected money from spectators, and made a profit. While a student at Harvard he and a friend bought a tour bus and organized tours of Boston, netting $10,000 over two summers.

But although Joe had attended Harvard, as an Irish Catholic he was not accepted into any of the final year clubs that would have allowed him to enter elite Boston society. The United States may have been the land of opportunity, but the Anglo elites descended from the early settlers ensured that parvenus were kept in line. Nowhere was this more true than in Boston, where the "Brahmin" Yankee elite controlled the major banks and brokerage houses. As the local joke had it, "The Lowells speak only to the Cabots and the Cabots speak only to God."

Determined to make his fortune in banking, in 1912 Joe started work as a clerk at Columbia Trust, a tiny Boston bank that his father and fifteen friends had set up. From there he soon landed a job as a Massachusetts bank examiner, and came to learn that Columbia Trust was the target of a takeover bid. He flew into action, borrowing enough to buy 51% of the bank's shares and thwart the takeover. The bank's president resigned and Joe took his place, becoming, aged twenty-five, the youngest bank president in Boston, if not the country.

For seven years Joe had been wooing Rose, the Mayor's daughter. Now that Joe's star was rising, and Honey Fitz's fast falling, the Mayor was no longer able to forestall Rose's marriage to the son of a man he despised. The young couple borrowed to buy a house in the Protestant Brookline district of Boston and a Model T Ford, and they hired a maid.

He had a rather narrow face and his ears stuck out a little bit and his hair wouldn't stay put, and all that added, I suppose, to an elfin quality in his appearance. But he was a very active, very lively little elf, full of energy when he wasn't ill and full of charm and imagination.

Rose Kennedy

Left: **Brookline, Massachusetts, 1917**
Jack, aged six months

A distant mother

All the Kennedys were blocked, totally blocked emotionally. Knowing the old man and Mrs. Kennedy, spending so much time in the house, I can readily see the limitations. Mrs. Kennedy, for all her kids, was not a mother ... And the old man—having his mistresses at the house for lunch and supper! I couldn't understand it! It was unheard of!

Betty Coxe Spalding, friend of Kathleen Kennedy

Rose Kennedy grew up the apple of her father's eye, pretty, intelligent, well educated, and capable. When she was seven, Honey Fitz took her with him to meet President McKinley in the White House, and by the time she was seventeen she was a local celebrity. When, however, her father lost his re-election bid for Mayor in 1907 under suspicion of corruption, he took Rose and his second daughter on a tour of Europe, leaving them there for two lonely years to be educated by nuns in Holland. Four years later, back as Mayor, he again set off for Europe with his wife and Rose, leading a business delegation.

Rose got her own way by marrying Joe Kennedy against her father's wishes, but she was soon disillusioned. The marriage quickly unraveled; Joe was a compulsive womanizer from the start, doing little to hide his liaisons.

Right: **Boston, Massachusetts, October 7, 1914**
Wedding of Joseph Kennedy to Rose Fitzgerald.

After six years of marriage, and pregnant with her fourth child, Rose had had enough of his absences and philandering, and in 1920 returned to her father's house. But Honey Fitz sent her back to her husband three weeks later, to fulfill her Catholic duty.

From then on, Rose and Joe led increasingly separate lives, with Rose pretending not to notice her husband's infidelities. She consoled herself by traveling widely, often leaving the family in the care of servants. Jack once memorably protested: "Gee, you're a great mother to go away and leave your children alone."

Joe was also absent for much of the time, off making his fortune and chasing other women, while Rose was bearing and raising her large brood. She retreated into a strident religiosity, covering walls with prayers and pictures of saints. Aided by a retinue of servants that grew with the family's wealth, she monitored the well-being and discipline of her children with minute attention. But, the love having quickly gone out of her marriage, she proved incapable of providing her children with warmth and affection.

The marriage almost broke apart again in the late twenties when Joe had a very public affair with Gloria Swanson, the goddess of the silent screen; but this did not prevent Rose later from accompanying Joe and Swanson to Paris as if nothing were going on. Appearances were everything.

Left: **Boston, Massachusetts, c. 1919**
Rose Kennedy with (left to right) Joe Jr., Rosemary, and Jack.

Next page: **Family group, 1927**
From left to right: Jack, Joe Jr., Joe Sr., Rosemary, Rose, Eunice, and Kathleen.

A driven father

[The old Protestant patriciate] scorned Jack's father, Joe Kennedy, not because he was Irish and a Catholic, as he would have it, but because he was so exuberantly and successfully a crook.

Gore Vidal

Jack's father, Joe Sr., was an archetypal lone wolf of American business. Growing to maturity at a time when U.S. capitalism was entering its first great period of decadence, when millions would be reduced to starvation, he built one of the largest fortunes in the country by scheming, deceit, and fraud.

The only time Joe took on a significant management role, at a shipbuilding plant turning out military vessels in 1917, he proved unequal to the task. His first fortune was made as a stock swindler, using inside information and working as part of informal syndicates to manipulate stocks. His second fortune was made in Hollywood movie production and distribution, though when he tried to move into the artistic sphere with an early talkie he was a disaster and had to pull out of the industry. His third fortune was made bootlegging whisky in league with the criminal underworld during Prohibition.

Once Joe had made enough to leave a million to each of his nine children, and then some, he set his sights on political power, or, rather, what he quaintly liked to refer to as "public service." As one of the wealthiest men backing the Democratic Party he was able to maneuver for political appointments once Franklin D Roosevelt became President in 1932. In a classic poacher-turned-gamekeeper move, FDR made Joe chairman of the Securities and Exchange

Commission, a newly created body charged with cleaning up business practices in the financial services industry.

But Joe hankered after a cabinet post. Failing to secure one, he got himself appointed U.S. Ambassador to the UK. No doubt FDR reckoned that would at least keep him out of the way—he had told Treasury secretary Henry Morgenthau "He's too dangerous to allow around here." But Joe's open admiration for Hitler, contempt for the British, and unshakeable conviction that Britain would be crushed in the coming war with Germany, were not the most appropriate opinions for the ambassador to America's closest ally in 1938.

FDR soon started to bypass Joe, developing instead a back channel to Winston Churchill, who was not even a cabinet minister at the time. Meanwhile Joe was continuing to use inside information he was acquiring as ambassador to make money.

Joe was from his early days a consummate master of public relations, which meant then, as now, that he used his wealth and influence to suborn, cajole and otherwise threaten journalists and editors to move public opinion the way he wanted. It has been alleged that when he was campaigning for his ambassador's post, he was privately paying Arthur Krock, the Washington Bureau Chief of the *New York Times,* $25,000 a year to promote him. When a critical article was about to appear in *Fortune* magazine in September 1937, Joe had it quashed by the editor and turned into a sympathetic profile. Drew Pearson of the *New York Daily Mirror* was another journalist who is said to have taken the Kennedy dollar.

The presentational skills Joe learned during his time in the movie industry failed to secure him the political career he craved; in Roosevelt he had met a man even more ruthless and wily than himself. But they later proved the key to launching his second son's political career, and his run for the presidency.

(Joe) told people that he himself was a caterpillar. His sons would be his butterflies.

Richard Mahoney

Right: **Place unknown, 1919**
Joe Sr., with his eldest sons, Joe Jr. (left) and Jack.

A sickly boy

From very young, Jack's health was poor. In fact it became a sort of legend. As his friend LeMoyne "Lem" Billings commented: "We used to joke about the fact that if I ever wrote a biography, I would call it *John F. Kennedy: A Medical History*. Yet I seldom ever heard him complain."

Apart from the usual illnesses of childhood, he suffered from an extraordinary array of ailments, many of them arcane and undiagnosed. With the hindsight of modern medical knowledge, and greater understanding of the effects of psychological stress on the immune system, one has to suspect that many of his problems had their origins in acute family tensions.

Three months before his third birthday he caught scarlet fever during an epidemic that was sweeping Boston. Later he had chicken pox, ear infections, continuous colds, and mumps. In 1930, when he was thirteen, the first year he was away at boarding school, he was laid low by an undiagnosed illness, and lost six pounds in the last three months of the year. He was desperately lonely. His father rarely visited, and his mother never at all. The following spring he collapsed with abdominal pains, and was diagnosed with appendicitis. Suffering constant fatigue, he failed to gain weight and was often unable to play sports.

Right: **Date and place unknown**
Jack with a pet dog.

At the beginning of 1933 Jack displayed "flu-like" symptoms, and complained of pains in his knees. A year later he was rushed to hospital suffering from hives and weight loss, and the doctors feared leukemia. His nickname at this time was "Rat Face." Although six foot tall, he was painfully thin and weighed only 125 pounds. During this period he was diagnosed with irritable bowel syndrome, and there began a series of treatments in Boston's Lahey Clinic and the Mayo Clinic in Rochester, Minnesota, which continued throughout his life. Jack's case would today be understood as related to the emotional stress he suffered: a lonely boy, feeling unloved, under strong pressure from his father to succeed, and locked into a competition with his elder brother that he could not win. It is likely that his immune system was weakened by depression.

The year Jack spent at Princeton university was a washout. Late enrolling after falling ill in London over the summer of 1935, he attended for a mere six weeks before he was forced to leave to take care of his health. To recuperate, his father sent him to work as a ranch hand in Arizona, near the Mexican border. After a month of hard physical work, and away from the pressures of family, he returned much fitter and stronger than at any time since he was first sent off to school.

Starting college again, this time at Harvard, he continued to be afflicted by irritable bowel syndrome and other problems, but nevertheless was able to swim, play golf, and sail, and even played some football in his first two years. But by the time he graduated at the age of twenty-three a bad back was added to his woes—and also venereal disease. He was successfully treated at the Lahey Clinic in 1940 for gonorrhea, but continued to suffer from urethritis, inflammation of the genitals, and discomfort in the region of the bladder and prostate.

My (white) blood count this morning was 3500. When I came it was 6000. At 1500 you die. They call me "2000 to go Kennedy."

In his brother's shadow

The home Jack grew up in was prosperous from the start, but was lacking in emotional warmth. Although Joe adored his children and developed close bonds with them all, he was a domineering father. He pushed them, particularly the boys, to succeed in sports, at their studies and as leaders in the making. They grew up loving him, yet suffering under the constant pressure to win his respect. To come second, he would tell them, was to fail.

Apart from his parents, the most important person in Jack's early life was his elder brother, Joe Jr. By the time Jack appeared in the world, Joe Sr. had already decided that Joe Jr. would be the one to carry forward the dynasty he was planning—as President of the United States. Joe Jr. was robust and respectful of authority, always seeking his father's approval. Jack, however, suffered from poor health his whole life, and struggled to keep up with an elder brother he admired and to whom he was intensely loyal, but whose shadow he was forever trying to escape.

In 1927, when Jack was ten, the family moved to a house overlooking the Hudson river in Riverdale, in the Bronx suburb of New York. They also bought an estate at Hyannis Port on Cape Cod, where they spent their summers. In 1929 they moved again, from Riverdale to Bronxville, to a mansion standing in six acres.

Left: **Hyannis Port, Cape Cod, Massachusetts, 1925**
Joe Jr. (left), aged nine, and Jack, aged seven.

An elite education

Jack was first sent to a day school in Riverdale, but at the age of thirteen he was packed off to a desolate Catholic boarding school, Canterbury School in New Milford, Connecticut. He was homesick, and while excelling at English and history he struggled with Latin and science. The following year he joined Joe Jr. at Choate School in Wallingford, Connecticut.

As the United States emerged as an imperialist power at the end of the nineteenth century, the east coast elites established private boarding schools in imitation of the English public schools. Choate was one of these, and strongly Protestant—Joe Sr. hoped that attendance there would help his sons break through the social restrictions that held him back, despite his growing wealth.

Whereas Joe Jr. made his way at Choate as an athlete and conformist, Jack was a popular rebel, an iconoclast testing the rules of the adult world. The headmaster referred to pupils who defied the rules as "mockers," so in his final year Jack and several of his friends organized a Muckers Club and got a local jeweler to make a 22 carat gold badge in the form of a shovel, which they all wore on their vests.

Previous page: **Hyannis Port, Cape Cod, Massachusetts, 1931**
From left to right: Bobby, Jack, Eunice, Jean, Joe Sr., Rose, Patricia, Kathleen, Joe Jr., and Rosemary.

Right: **Choate School, Connecticut, June, 1935**
After graduating from Choate, Jack followed Lem Billings to Princeton but transferred to Harvard the following year.

For this Jack came close to being expelled—Joe was even summoned to the school by the irate headmaster. To Jack's relief, his father was rather proud of him, telling him that "If that crazy Muckers Club had been mine, you can be sure it wouldn't have started with an M!"

Joe Jr. had gone on to study at Harvard, so when he left Choate in 1935 Jack opted to follow Lem Billings, his closest school friend, to Princeton. But he spent much of that year with undiagnosed health problems, and decided to transfer to Harvard the following year.

During his first two years at Harvard his main interests were in sports and socializing. He tried hard at football, but although he made it onto the freshman team, at six foot and only 150 pounds he was too frail to make the grade. At swimming, however, he excelled, and his team won all its events.

Jack's friend Torbert Macdonald recalled one time when Jack had flu, but was desperate to make the team. "So every day I'd sneak into the infirmary with some food for him. As soon as he'd eaten, we'd slip out the back door, and I'd drive him to the indoor athletic building, where he'd doggedly practice his backstroke."

Left: **Harvard College, Cambridge, Massachusetts, March 10, 1938**
Practicing for the college swimming team.

I have no first-hand knowledge of the depression. My family had one of the great fortunes of the world and it was worth more than ever then. We had bigger houses, more servants, we traveled more ... I really did not learn about the depression until I read about it at Harvard ...

Right: **Palm Beach, April, 1936**
From left to right: Lem Billings and Jack with Bobby; Patricia Kennedy is in the foreground.

Next page: **Southampton, England, July 2, 1938**
Joe Sr. with his eldest sons, Joe Jr. and Jack, returning to his posting as Ambassador to London, on the French liner *Normandie*.

I know more about the European situation than anybody else, and it's up to me to see that the country gets it ... There's no sense in our getting in. We'd just be holding the bag ... What would we be fighting for? ... Democracy is finished in England. It may be here ... Hitler has all the ports in Europe, you see ... It is a practical question, how much (aid) to send ... It is a question of how long England can hold out. If she collapses soon, then stop.

Joseph P. Kennedy, November 10, 1940

Left: **London, 1939**
Jack with his father, now Ambassador to Britain, en route from London to Rome for the coronation of Pope Pius XII.

International travels

Although Joe Jr., as the first born, was chosen by his father for grooming from early years for high political office, Joe Sr. equally encouraged his second son to be interested in public affairs, and particularly in international affairs. Jack responded enthusiastically, and he read widely during the long periods of childhood and adolescence he spent in bed with various ailments. Winston Churchill was an early hero—Jack read his books throughout his life.

Jack got his first opportunity to visit Europe in the summer of 1937,when he was twenty, at the end of his first year at Harvard. He shipped a brand new Ford convertible to Le Havre, on the French coast, and, with his devoted friend Lem Billings in tow, set off on a tour through France, Italy, Austria, Germany, and the Netherlands, ending in England. Their main interests seem to have consisted in visiting cathedrals, attempting to take the political pulse of the countries they visited, and bedding women—the latter more in the case of Jack than of Billings, who by all accounts was more interested in bedding Jack.

Jack's diary entries didn't get much beyond describing national stereotypes of each country, the bloodthirsty Spaniards, the disciplined Germans, and so on. His conclusion that "fascism is the thing for Germany and Italy, communism for Russia, and democracy for America and England" does not suggest he had yet developed any great understanding of social structures or political systems.

Right: **The Hague, Netherlands, August 24, 1937**
Jack (left) with Lem Billings and a dachshund acquired during their summer vacation in Europe. But the pet had to go when it transpired that Jack was allergic to dog fur.

His journal does, however, show that he was developing an inquisitiveness and a sense of detachment from what he was observing, a quality which became acutely developed by the time he became President.

In December 1937 Joe Sr. finally succeeded in having Roosevelt appoint him Ambassador to the Court of Saint James, that is, to London. The following summer Jack worked in the embassy, and developed a taste for socializing with the English aristocracy. His sister Kathleen, to whom of all the siblings he felt the closest, became so involved with English upper class life that she married the Marquis of Hartington, heir to Chatsworth House in Derbyshire, one of the grandest estates in the country.

In March 1939 Jack was back in London. He accompanied his parents to Rome for the coronation of Pope Pius XII, stopping off at the U.S. Embassy in Paris on the way back. Fanny Holtzmann, a lawyer from New York who was in Europe trying to help primarily Jewish refugees leave for the United States, bumped into Joe Jr. and Jack in the London embassy's visa department. She recounts how Jack gave her an idea for getting round the technicalities of obtaining long-term visas, and may have helped her save hundreds of lives. "Why not give them all temporary visas to attend the World's Fair in New York? It's running out of customers."

In May, with war only four months away, he was off again, alone, on another tour of Europe, and then ventured as far as the Middle East. The aim of the trip was to gather information for his senior thesis in politics the following year.

Left: **London, 1937**
Jack recovering from jaundice in hospital at the end of his summer trip through Europe with Lem Billings.

His journey took him to Danzig and Warsaw, then to Leningrad, Moscow, Kiev, Bucharest, Istanbul, Jerusalem, Beirut, Damascus and Athens. In August he was off again, joining his family on the French Riviera, where Marlene Dietrich and her daughter were frequent companions, then on to Germany, Italy and Czechoslovakia, which was already under German occupation. He was back in London in September, in time to accompany his family to the visitors' gallery of the House of Commons to hear Prime Minister Neville Chamberlain declare war on Germany:

"This morning the British Ambassador in Berlin handed the German Government a final note stating that unless we heard from them by eleven o'clock that they were prepared at once to withdraw their troops from Poland, a state of war would exist between us. I have to tell you that no such understanding has been received and that consequently this country is at war with Germany."

Right: **Westminster, London, September 3, 1939**
Joe Jr., Kathleen, and Jack on their way to a special sitting of the House of Commons at which Prime Minister Neville Chamberlain declared war on Germany following the invasion of Poland by Hitler's armies.

I didn't see much of his serious side, and indeed, at that date—well of course he was twenty, twenty-one, and I was about the same age—perhaps neither of us had a very serious side to be seen at that moment ... I didn't detect it, although he must have been more interested than I thought, because of course he was preparing his book *Why England Slept*.

David Ormsby-Gore, later Lord Harlech

Right: **New York, March, 1939**

Just back from Berlin and London, Jack reads about the German invasion of Czechoslovakia. His father had advised anyone who would listen in the British government not to oppose Hitler. He arranged for Charles Lindbergh, the U.S. aviator subsequently decorated by Hitler, to meet top officials of the British Air Force, to explain that German air superiority was so overwhelming that it could bomb any European city with impunity.

A critical intelligence

Jack's final year at Harvard coincided with the first year of the war, and he spent much of it preparing his final thesis, an attempt to explain why England was not prepared for war when it came. He could have argued that the country had in fact spent the past decade building up its air force, producing the Spitfires and Hurricanes which proved decisive in repelling the attempted German invasion of 1942. However, he chose to argue that rearmament had been thwarted by the democratic system, because none of the groups within the society were prepared to make the financial sacrifices necessary.

There is nothing populist about this early analysis. What it shows is a young man preoccupied by a conflict among European elites, and the system of government most appropriate for furthering their ends. Democracy, he writes, may be "a 'pleasanter' form of government", but "it is not the best form of government for meeting the present world problem."

Returning from Europe in October, 1939, Jack had proposed in an editorial in the Harvard magazine *Crimson* that Roosevelt should negotiate peace with Germany, allowing Hitler a free hand in Eastern Europe and a share of overseas colonies, essentially the line taken by his father and his elder brother, Joe Jr. However, in the thesis he went on to write he began to distance himself from his father's views, accommodating his position to the policies Roosevelt was starting to promote.

Through the influence of his father, and with the editorial help of New York Times columnist Arthur Krock and an introduction from *TIME* and *LIFE* publisher Henry Luce, Jack was able to publish his thesis as a book. Its title, *Why England Slept*, was a deliberate echo of Churchill's title *While England Slept*. Sales seem to have been substantial. If so, it was in large part due to bulk purchases made by Joe Sr.

In the spring of 1941, Jack sailed with his mother and his sister Eunice on a trip to Latin America, and while in Argentina they stayed with the influential Carcano family. He had already been called up for military service, but had failed his physical examinations. It was not until October of that year that he was accepted as a naval ensign—and then only after the intervention of Joe Sr. Even so, he did not enter combat until March 1943, when he was sent to the Solomon Islands in the Pacific.

Following the death of his brother Joe Jr. during the last phase of the war, the Kennedy political mantle fell on Jack's shoulders. In April, 1945, his father arranged for him to be sent to San Francisco by the Hearst owned *Chicago Herald-American*, to cover the gathering of world politicians that created the United Nations. He was decidedly not optimistic about the likelihood of the UN being able to resolve international disputes. Later, as President, he was to ignore it completely during the most dangerous crisis the world has ever faced, the Cuban Missile Crisis of October 1962.

From San Francisco, Hearst newspapers sent Kennedy to London to cover the General Election of July 1945, which saw his political hero Winston Churchill lose to a reforming Labour Party, despite Churchill's venerable status as war leader. Kennedy found Labour uncongenial and authoritarian.

After a trip to Ireland, where he met President Eamon De Valera, Kennedy traveled to Paris. Here he was invited by James Forrestal, Secretary of the Navy and a friend of his father, who had already marked Jack as a promising young man to promote in the world of politics, to accompany him to Berlin.

Becoming his own man

Before sacking Joe, FDR put him under surveillance by both the FBI and the Secret Service, who soon confirmed that Joe was hatching a plot with Marshall Pétain, the head of the collaborationist Vichy government of Nazi occupied France. Joe had sent an emissary to see both Pétain and Hitler, to sound them out about a negotiated peace between Germany and Britain.

Joe already had a reputation as a draft dodger in 1917, and as a vicious anti-semite. Now he not only supported U.S. isolation from the storms brewing in Europe and the Far East, but he was revealed as a potential collaborator with the Nazi regime in conflict with the administration he served. His views were shared by many other members of the U.S. elite—Senator Prescott Bush (grandfather of President George Bush), Averell Harriman and the Dulles brothers, Alan and John Foster, for example—but unlike Joe they were not administration appointees at the time.

While Joe Jr. endorsed his father's views and was active in the anti-interventionist movement at Harvard, Jack was embarrassed. His recent book on British Prime Minister Neville Chamberlain's appeasement of Hitler, *Why England Slept*, was less dogmatic, and by the time Joe gave his notorious interview to the *Boston Globe* in November 1940 he was fully behind F. D. Roosevelt, convinced that the U.S. would have to enter the war.

Right: **Harvard College, Boston, Massachusetts, c. 1940**
Jack working on his final undergraduate thesis *Why England Slept,* in which he started to distance himself from his father's strong pro-German appeasement views. With much help from his father and friends of his father, the thesis was later published as a book.

This young man is a very sort of rough American youth but he's very bright, he's very intelligent ... And one day he says he's going to be president—and I wouldn't be surprised if one day he isn't, because he's got a very inquisitive intelligence!

Senora Chiquita Carcano

Left: **Rio de Janciro, May, 1941**
Jack with his mother Rose and sister Eunice on a vacation trip to South America. In Argentina, where he stayed with the Carcano family whose head was the Argentinian ambassador to Vichy France, he learned that pro-German feeling was strong.

The making of a hero

When the government announced a military draft in October 1940, Jack immediately registered, and his number came up eighteenth in the whole country. Having finished at Harvard in the summer, he had just the previous month enrolled in political science and business courses at the University of Stanford, California.

In his eagerness to enlist, Jack no doubt wanted to avoid the opprobrium that his father had suffered as a World War I draft dodger, but he had also come to recognize—unlike his father and elder brother—that military support of Britain was essential to defending U.S. national interests. In any case, the likelihood of the Army accepting him, given his perilous state of health seemed remote: "They will never take me in the Army. And yet if I don't go, it will look quite bad."

He tried several times to pass the physical examinations, without success. Then in June 1941, Joe Jr., having become a leader on American campuses of the isolationists who opposed American entry into the war, shocked everyone by enlisting in the Naval Reserve. At this point sibling rivalry seems to have kicked in, spurring Jack to call on the help of a Rear Admiral who had formerly been naval attaché at the U.S. embassy in London. By August, he too had been admitted into the Naval Reserve.

There followed desk jobs in Washington and Charleston, and then combat training in the Great Lakes, Rhode Island and Florida. Although in constant pain from his back and other ailments, he had determination and plenty of experience of sailing in his youth.

Right: **Palm Beach, Florida, May 4, 1942**
Jack (left) with his brother Joe Jr. after they had been called up for the navy.

He qualified with high marks in everything from gunnery to navigation. In March 1943, two and a half years after he was called up, he was finally sent into a war zone, in the South Pacific.

While undergoing training, the opportunity arose to join a group preparing to sail PT torpedo boats. These were fast, plywood-hulled eighty-foot boats, designed to make surprise attacks on larger vessels. In reality, in a war dominated by air attack, massive warships and submarines, the PT boats were an anachronism. They used highly inflammable aviation fuel, had no armor plating, and were equipped with guns which were scarcely more powerful than rifles. They were used for night time operations and, since they did not have radar and couldn't use lights for fear of giving away their position, navigation was a challenge.

Nevertheless, PT boats offered Jack the chance to have his own command, even if only over a dozen men. His unhappy schooling, combined with his mother's loveless obsession with rules, had left him with a lifelong aversion to discipline. Command of a PT boat offered the romance of individual glory he would have been unlikely to find as a member of the crew of a large ship.

He finally got his wish on April 25, 1943, when he took command of PT 109 in the Solomon Islands. In July, he several times came close to being bombed by Japanese planes. Then, at 2.00 a.m. on Monday, August 2, whether by accident or design, a Japanese destroyer rammed Kennedy's boat, sheering off one side and leaving two of the crew of thirteen dead, and several others badly wounded.

Although PT 109's position was obvious from the spilled kerosene burning on the water, the squadron commander assumed it had sunk without trace and did not mount a search. In fact, Kennedy and the other ten survivors jumped into the sea and waited for the Japanese to disappear. They spent the day hanging onto the wreckage, then decided in the evening to swim to an island. Jack towed one of his crew, Pappy McMahon, who was badly burned, by holding the straps of his life jacket between his teeth. Four hours later they reached the island, which turned out to have neither water nor food. Later that evening Kennedy swam back out with a blinking light to try to attract the attention of a passing PT boat, returning only at noon the next day. On Wednesday, the 4th, Jack led his crew to another island where they found coconuts, again towing Pappy McMahon. The next day he swam to yet another island with Ross Barney, and happened on crackers, candy and water, left behind by some Japanese.

Returning to the island where the rest of the crew were waiting, they met two islanders, who showed Kennedy how to scratch a message inside the husk of a coconut, which they then took in their canoe to an Allied base. On Saturday, six days after their ordeal began, they were rescued by a party of British sailors.

Despite his continuing poor health, Jack refused the opportunity of returning to the United States, and instead took command of another PT boat. But once again his activities amounted to little, in common with the entire PT boat operation.

By November his health had collapsed once more. He was diagnosed with a duodenal ulcer and chronic disc disease of the lower back. He returned to San Francisco on January 7, 1944, his combat service having lasted less than six months.

Although Jack did not see himself as a hero, the family publicity machine quickly moved into action. Within days an extensive account of his exploits appeared on the front page of the *Boston Globe* headlined: *"Tells Story of PT Epic: Kennedy Lauds Men, Disdains Hero Stuff."*

It was absolutely involuntary. They sank my boat.

on being asked how he became a war hero

Left: **Solomon Islands, South Pacific, 1943**
Jack aboard the U.S.S. PT 109 which he commanded. This was an 80-foot plywood torpedo vessel capable of 40 knots, but prone to mechanical problems.

John Hersey, a friend who had married one of Jack's ex girlfriends, was intrigued by the story of PT 109 as a tale of survival. He interviewed Jack at length about the episode, but when his article was rejected by *LIFE*, and instead published by *The New Yorker*, Joe Sr. was not impressed. He wanted mass circulation, so he persuaded *Reader's Digest* to publish a condensed article. He then promptly ignored the contract and himself printed tens of thousands of copies for private distribution.

During his stint in the South Seas, Jack demonstrated a capacity for leadership that had always been latent; he became his own man, separating himself for the first time from the domineering presence of his father. His time adrift after his boat was sunk revealed him to have a strong instinct to survive, and remarkable physical tenacity, despite his dreadful physical condition and the constant pain he suffered.

All this proved too much for Joe Jr. as he saw his younger brother, already a successfully published author, being fêted as a war hero. Moreover, Jack was beginning to display a mercurial charm which drew people of all kinds toward him, a talent of enormous political potential which the more plodding Joe completely lacked. Joe confided to an English friend that he had come to believe that Jack, not he, was destined to become president. Joe, by contrast, and despite his undoubted courage, had proved to be a pilot of only average ability, flying transports and patrol planes, with little prospect of winning a medal.

Right: **South Pacific, 1943**
A skeletal Jack Kennedy, looking more like a prisoner-of-war than a torpedo boat commander.

When his thirty missions were up, he volunteered for ten more, and then for even more. He finally volunteered for a mission of quite extraordinary danger for which, if he had succeeded, he would have won the Navy Cross, the highest naval honor.

On August 12th, 1944, Joe set off across the English Channel in a plane loaded with some ten tons of TNT, making it a flying bomb. The target was a German emplacement near Calais—Joe and his co-pilot were to bail out over the sea, while his plane continued its course under radio control from two planes flying behind. In the event, the plane exploded before it was anywhere near its target. No remains of Joe's body were found.

On hearing the news, Joe Sr.'s life and ambitions collapsed around him. For a man thwarted in his own overweening ambition to become president, he could only reconstruct his life by transferring his ambition from his first to his second son.

We can only imagine the complex emotions Jack must have felt at the death of the brother he so adored and venerated, yet who, since his earliest years, had placed him under such pressure to succeed that his frail body was constantly on the point of collapse.

While Joe Sr.'s grief was beyond expression, Jack expressed his by preparing a monument to his brother in the form of a small book entitled *As we Remember Joe*, in a limited edition of five hundred copies. With this memorial, Jack buried Joe, escaped the hold of his monstrous family, and opened the way to his own political career. From now on his father would be the instrument of his success. The child had become father of the man.

Right: **South Pacific, 1943**
Jack drinking tea with an unidentified woman.

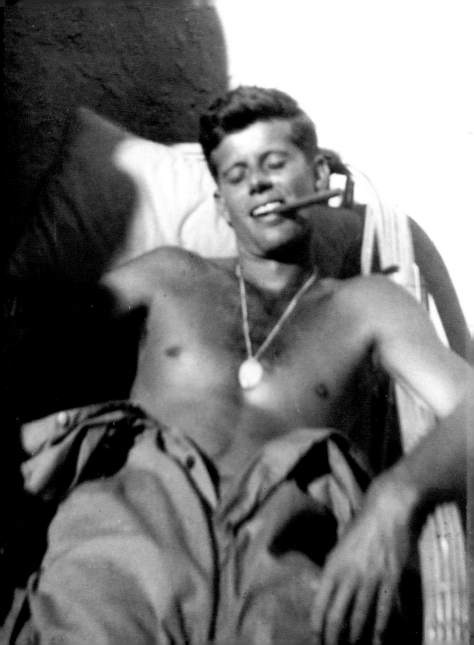

He had extraordinary energy. He just wouldn't give up. He just had to have something happening. That's what made him go out and try to flag down a PT boat.

Gerard Zinser, member of PT 109 crew

...ascism. Embarra... ...ain it away, but in fact this private observation ...oright shaft of light onto the attitudes of the political world which Jack was being groomed. Joe Sr. was strongly anti-emitic, like many in his social circle. As U.S. ambassador to ...ndon he had attempted to negotiate a secret deal with Hitler, a an for whom he had considerable admiration. He had launched

Previous page: **Hyannis Port, Cape Cod, Massachusetts, 1944**
Relaxing at the family house with his sisters.

Left: **Palm Beach, Florida, February 1944**
Jack was a subscriber to the James Dean brand of narcissism before James Dean was even heard of.

Any man who may be asked in this century what he did to make his life worthwhile, I think can respond with a good deal of pride and satisfaction, "I served in the United States Navy."

Right: **Chelsea Naval Hospital, Massachusetts, June 12, 1944**
Kennedy receives his Marine Corps medal for Gallantry in Action, "for heroism in the rescue of 3 men following the ramming and sinking of his motor torpedo boat while attempting a torpedo attack on a Japanese destroyer in the Solomon Islands area on the night of August 1–2, 1943."

Visiting the ruins of the Reich

Visiting Germany in August 1945 with U.S. Navy Secretary James Forrestal, Jack witnessed the terrible devastation of the cities. They saw the ruins of Hitler's bunker in Berlin, where Hitler and Eva Braun had committed suicide as the city was smashed by the Allied bombardment, and witnessed the Soviet troops asserting control in the eastern zone. In Frankfurt, he went to Eisenhower's headquarters, then on to Austria to see Hitler's Eagle's Nest, high above Berchtesgaden, near Salzburg. He noted in his diary of 1945 that:

... within a few years Hitler will emerge from the hatred that surrounds him now as one of the most significant figures who ever lived. He had boundless ambition for his country which rendered him a menace to the peace of the world, but he had a mystery about him in the way that he lived and in the manner of his death that will live and grow after him. He had in him the stuff of which legends are made.

Jack's comment comes as a shock. All the more so since he was by this time twenty-eight years old, a veteran of a world war supposedly fought against f———————ssed commentators have sought to expla——————
throws a——

Jack's political career by asking his old friend William Randolph Hearst—the epitome of the right wing newspaper tycoon, immortalized in Orson Welles' film *Citizen Kane*—to give him hands-on experience as a political journalist.

Forrestal was also a friend of Joe Sr., and the trip to Germany was intended to give Jack insight into foreign policy-making at the epicenter where the new world order of the Cold War was being established. President Truman was staying near Berlin and preparing for the Potsdam peace conference. It was here he took the decision to drop hydrogen bombs on Nagasaki and Hiroshima.

Forrestal, who later became Truman's Defence Secretary, was former president of the merchant bank Dillon, Read, which had specialized in loans to Germany. He was a member of a small elite of U.S. bankers and lawyers that had had business links with Germany since the 1920s.

Others in this elite circle included Averell Harriman, of Brown Brothers, later a member of Kennedy's administration; Senator Prescott Bush, father of George Bush I and grandfather of President George W. Bush; and John Foster Dulles, head of the Sullivan & Cromwell law firm which maintained an office in Berlin throughout the war and represented leading Germany companies. Clients included the chemical company I.G. Farben, which supplied the Zyklon-B poison gas that was used in the concentration camps. Dulles was later Secretary of State under Eisenhower, while his brother Allen Dulles was director of the CIA.

During the years of Hitler's rise to power, Forrestal was one of the key figures involved in formulating U.S. policy toward Europe. This dominant foreign policy elite regarded Nazi Germany as the main bulwark against the Soviet Union extending its influence into Western Europe.

Hitler was appreciated by the State Department as the man who could destroy working class organizations in Germany and save capitalism. The shift toward seeing Nazi Germany, Japan and Italy as the enemy only came as Hitler began to challenge U.S. economic interests.

One of the visits Forrestal arranged with Jack was to the I. G. Farben plant in Frankfurt. It is interesting to note Kennedy's diary entry: "We drove to the Farben building which was completely untouched, though surrounded by ruins." Had the company deliberately been spared by Allied bombing?

As Defense Secretary under Truman, Forrestal was to oversee the creation of the post-war military-industrial complex, and laid the basis for Cold War confrontation with the Soviet Union. He committed suicide in 1949 during a paranoid nervous breakdown. Clearly a man who took his work too seriously, he believed he was being pursued by a vast conspiracy of communists and Jews.

Jack's youthful comments on Hitler are probably no more than an echo of what he had heard discussed over dinner during his trip. Hitler had proved to be dispensable once his ambitions diverged from U.S. interests. Over the years since, many other tyrants have trodden the same path from trusted U.S. friend to mortal foe.

Left: **Berlin, August, 1945**
Navy Secretary James Forrestal (left), who invited Jack to accompany him on his trip to Germany.

chapter 2

From soldier
to statesman

The road to power 1945–1960

Even before Kennedy returned from Europe in August, 1945, his Boston campaign was already under way, with Joe Sr. and his grandfather, Honey Fitz, out giving speeches. Soon national profiles of Kennedy began to appear in *TIME* and *LIFE* magazines. The sitting Democratic congressman for the Eleventh District, Michael Curley, under federal investigation for mail fraud, was persuaded to step aside and campaign instead for mayor.

Honey Fitz set about assembling a political team. But it was Joe Sr. who master-minded the campaign, spending as much as half a million dollars to buy up all billboards and poster sites and encourage supporters of rival candidates to desert. Kennedy, as president of the Joseph P. Kennedy, Jr. Foundation, handed over to Cardinal Cushing a check for $600,000 for the poor children of Boston. Joe Sr. had copies of the *Reader's Digest* account of Kennedy's PT 109 heroics distributed to every household.

However, Kennedy's own furious efforts played a part in his success too, though he was in poor health most of the time. He campaigned under the slogan "The New Generation Offers a Leader," and proved particularly adept at attracting women voters. He won the nomination with nearly twice the number of votes as his nearest rival, and the seat itself with a margin of nearly three to one.

Previous page: **Washington D.C.**
Jack and Jackie posing in front of the Stars and Stripes.

Right: **City Hall, Boston, Massachusetts, April 23, 1946**
Aged 28, Kennedy files his first nomination papers with election commissioner Joseph Langone. He was to win a seat in Congress.

I got Jack into politics. I was the one. I told him Joe was dead and that it was therefore his responsibility to run for Congress. Jack didn't want to ...

Joe Kennedy

Previous page: **Charlestown, Massachusetts, June 1946**
Kennedy marches in the Bunker Hill Day Parade, as he campaigns for a seat in the U.S. Congress.

Left: **Boston, Massachusetts, 1946**
The men behind Kennedy's political career; his grandfather, John F (Honey Fitz) Fitzgerald, was a former Mayor of Boston and U.S. Congressman; his father, Joseph P Kennedy, was a former U.S. Ambassador to London.

It was like being drafted. My father wanted his eldest son in politics. "Wanted" isn't the right word. He demanded it, you know my father.

Right: **Bellevue Hotel, Boston, Massachusetts, September 1946**
Campaigning for Congress. Photos of his parents are on the shelf behind Kennedy.

Next page: **Boston, Massachusetts, June 19, 1946**
Kennedy with his parents Rose and Joe, and his grandparents Josie and Honey Fitz, after winning the Democratic Primary for the Massachusetts Eleventh Congressional District.

A new boy in the House

During his five years as a representative, Kennedy did not achieve very much in the way of legislation. But that was not really the point. The House he entered was heavily dominated by the Republicans, and short of spending long years waiting for seniority there was not a lot he could have accomplished.

Instead he spent his time preparing for the next step in his political career. He had a large staff, paid for by his father, in both his Boston and his Washington offices, and was free from mundane duties. He turned thirty during his first year in the House, but showed no interest in marrying and settling down. He shared a small house with his sister Eunice in the elegant Georgetown district of Washington, and led an active social life.

The central theme of Kennedy's political life was already well honed. In a radio broadcast during the final weeks of his election campaign he recalled his response to a question he had been asked about the Soviet threat at a political meeting:

I told them that Soviet Russia today is a slave state of the worst sort. I told them that Soviet Russia is embarked upon a program of world aggression. I told them that the freedom-loving countries of the world must stop Soviet Russia now, or be destroyed.

On the home front, Kennedy championed the right of labor unions to join in free collective bargaining—this was a popular cause in the working class district he represented. He was, however, fiercely opposed to communist infiltration of organized labor, and joined the sub-committee whose mission it was to root it out.

On economic matters Kennedy was a fiscal conservative, but he was by no means so rigidly doctrinaire as to imagine that free market capitalism could supply all social needs. He strongly championed federal subsidies for low cost housing for veterans and slum clearance. This did nothing to hurt his political appeal as a high profile veteran himself.

Behind the scenes Joe Sr.'s PR machine kept his son in the public eye. The U.S. Junior Chamber of Commerce named Kennedy the most outstanding man of his generation for 1946, and there was a steady stream of newspaper articles and radio interviews.

Kennedy's health took a severe nose-dive during a trip to Europe in the summer of 1947. In London he was rushed to hospital, apparently close to death, and a priest came to pronounce the last rites. He was diagnosed with Addison's disease, which progressively destroys the adrenal glands. Back in the U.S. he was given a new treatment—cortisone injections—which probably saved his life. But he was also told he was unlikely to live more than ten to fifteen years. Medical evidence that has recently come to light shows that the bones in his spinal column were already collapsing at this time, perhaps under the influence of the steroid therapy.

In 1948 Kennedy embarked on a program of speaking engagements throughout Massachusetts, aiming to cover all 39 cities and 312 towns. Each weekend he would pack in meetings from breakfast to dinner, sometimes covering as many as 12 events in one day. The pain and discomfort was often excruciating.

He toyed with the idea of running for Governor, but backed off when opinion polls suggested he would have a tough fight on his hands. Instead, he decided to wait until the 1952 elections, finally deciding to run for the Senate instead of the State House.

The fervent anti-communist

Kennedy's early years in politics coincided with an intense debate within the U.S. elites as to how they should reorganise the world. America had emerged from the war with half of the world's wealth, as the indispensable superpower. They wanted to keep it that way.

Young Kennedy, as his father had always wished, was moving beyond his Boston Irish gilded ghetto in ways Joe Sr.—despite his wealth and posting as ambassador to London—never fully could. In the thirties Joe had championed isolationist retreat from Europe and accommodation with Nazi Germany. Now in the post-war years the same thinking led him to argue that America should rebuild its economy at home, and not go spending money on armaments and foreign aid programs. If Western Europe went communist for a generation, then so be it.

Joe's view was an extreme version of the approach championed by George Kennan, the foreign policy chief at the State Department who, like Joe, had championed Hitler's Germany as the core of an anti-Soviet Europe. Kennan believed that, with limited resources, the U.S. should choose carefully which battles it chose to fight.

During the Truman administration, Kennan's view lost out to the more radical approach of National Security Advisor Paul Nitze, who did not see resources as a constraint: as President Kennedy later expressed it, the American people should be prepared to "bear any burden." Nitze, formerly a colleague of Kennedy's mentor James Forrestal at Dillon, Read merchant bank, became the author of the key document of the Cold War, National Security Council Memorandum 68. This document, written in April 1950 but not declassified until 1975, explains that "the Cold War is in fact a real war in which the survival of the free world is at stake." Soviet

Russia, a "slave state", was bent on world domination and wanted to destroy America, made vulnerable by its tolerance, diversity and concern for the individual. America had to guard against communist infiltration of the labor unions, schools, churches, media … All the buzz words of Kennedy's early speeches are here.

Already in 1947 President Truman had proposed to Congress his "Truman Doctrine" that the U.S. should provide military and financial aid to any country facing a military threat from the Soviet Union. The first fruit of this policy was an aid request for $227 million to defend Italy from communism, which Kennedy supported.

Kennedy was at first less convinced when that same year Truman proposed the Marshall Plan, a massive $17 billion program of loans and grants designed to prevent a communist takeover of western Europe. He was also initially skeptical of the need to create NATO, the U.S.-dominated military alliance with western Europe, on the grounds that Asia was more important to U.S. interests and that Europe should be largely responsible for its own defense.

But he did sign up early to the anti-communist witch hunt at home, which began in 1946 with hysteria at supposed communist infiltration of the State Department and other government agencies. F.B.I. boss J. Edgar Hoover claimed there were more than one hundred thousand communists secretly at work. The House set up an Un-American Activities Committee and demanded that government employees take loyalty oaths.

When Joseph McCarthy, a Republican senator for Wisconsin, launched his Senate investigations into communists and fellow-travelers in 1953, he took Bobby Kennedy on as assistant counsel. But his zealous approach created too many enemies, and his colleagues eventually had to restrain him through a censure motion.

Kennedy clearly approved of the Senator's campaign, and there are even accounts of occasions when he lost his his habitual emotional control and exploded in McCarthy's defense. Earlier he had supported legislation requiring registration of communists, and providing for their internment during a national emergency.

It was not just that McCarthy was a family friend and fellow Irish Catholic who visited them at weekends. His politics coincided with a deep-seated Kennedy contempt for liberals. In his campaigning, however, Kennedy was careful to distance himself from McCarthy. He could not afford to gain a name as a scourge of civil liberties with an electorate containing so many labor unionists and liberal Jews.

After a trip to Europe in the fall of 1949, Kennedy told the Senate Foreign Relations Committee that "Europe is our first line of defense," and he became a leading advocate for Franco's Spain joining NATO.

During the fall of 1951 Kennedy, accompanied by Bobby and his sister Patricia, made a seven week trip to the Middle East and Asia. He returned even more convinced that the Cold War overshadowed all else, and fully endorsed the Marshall Plan and NATO.

In India Prime Minister Jawarhal Nehru explained patiently that war would not stop poor countries turning to communism, which was spreading because the western nations offered them nothing. In Indochina he saw that the French were losing their war against Ho Chi Minh's supporters who, he understood, were nationalists before they were communists. He came back convinced that the U.S. should confront communism in the Third World not just with arms but also with material aid and propaganda for the American way of life. Here were the seeds of the Alliance for Progress and the Peace Corps which he initiated as President.

Right: **Vietnam, November 1951**
In rear, with Gen. de Lattre de Tassigny, commander of the French forces

First Senate race

Once polling commissioned by his father showed he had a good chance of winning, Kennedy threw his hat into the ring for the Massachusetts Senate seat in 1952. His opponent was Henry Cabot Lodge Jr., scion of the leading "Boston Brahmin" family, who was first elected to the Senate in 1936. Lodge's father and Kennedy's maternal grandfather, Honey Fitz, had been personal and political enemies. If Kennedy could beat him, he would truly have arrived as a member of the nation's elite.

The Kennedy team invented a new style of campaigning. Those who had run his previous campaigns for the House were moved aside and Bobby came in as manager. At twenty-six years old, he proved himself completely focused and in control. And behind, controlling Bobby, was Joe.

On the political issues there was little to choose between the two candidates. They both championed the Marshall Plan, NATO and the need to oppose communism. When they debated, on radio and in front of a live audience, Kennedy had difficulty holding his ground against the more experienced man.

When Joe decided to try using television to promote Jack, the results were mixed. Alone in the studio, without a live audience, he found it hard to improvise. But in some broadcasts the charisma he would display later as President shone through.

Kennedy knew from the start that he had to appeal to every minority and ethnic group in the state, the way Honey Fitz had always done. The Irish Catholics he could count on, but the Jews presented a particular problem because of his father's widely known anti-semitism, and Lodge's strong support of the new state of Israel. But he won them round with the endorsement of Eleanor Roosevelt and her son, who were idolized by American Jews. He told them to remember it was him they were voting for, not his father.

To woo the black vote, Kennedy joined the National Association for the Advancement of Colored People and arranged large contributions to black charities. He sent his mother to speak French to the French speakers. The Italians he impressed with Italy's Star of Solidarity, awarded for his support for Italy's rearmament.

Kennedy's greatest success, however, was with female voters. His sisters and mother set about organizing tea parties, usually held on Sunday afternoons. There were thirty-five in all, with the most successful one attracting 5,500 women. Rose and her daughters also hosted two *Coffee with the Kennedys*— morning television programs, with viewers phoning in. Young women also flocked to work for the campaign, and Bobby was able to command a staff of around twenty-five thousand. They sent out 1.2 million brochures.

Underpinning everything was Joe's money. The Kennedy campaign is believed to have spent several million dollars, compared with the one million of the Lodge campaign. Perhaps most critically of all, Joe, knowing of the paper's financial difficulties, offered the *Boston Post* proprietor a loan of $500,000 to get him to switch his endorsement from Lodge to Kennedy.

In the event, Kennedy squeaked home by 70,000 votes. But in elections where a Democrat lost the state governorship and the Republican General Eisenhower beat Adlai Stevenson to the presidency, this was a stunning achievement.

Next page: **Television studio, 1952**
Jack with his mother and sisters in "Coffee with the Kennedys."

Bobby's baptism of fire

Bobby was the seventh child in the Kennedy family, and he always had to run to keep up. He lacked the charm of his elder brothers, and had to struggle for achievement in his studies and at sports. By nature he was taciturn and brusque with other people. Early on he developed a strong moralistic streak and, more than his siblings, inherited his mother's religious piety.

Bobby followed his father and his brothers to Harvard, where he barely scraped through academically and didn't integrate socially. Most of his time was spent on the football field, making up in determination what he lacked in size and skill.

While still at Harvard, Bobby took time out to work on his brother's 1946 campaign for the House of Representatives. When his grandfather Honey Fitz had campaigned for office, he had had all six brothers on his team, and now, at eighty-three, he was campaigning with his grandsons. No one in the family expected very much of Bobby, who didn't seem a natural canvasser. But he threw himself into the campaign with fervor, and at one point had to be restrained from knocking on doors after 10 P.M. Dave Powers, who would remain a close Kennedy aide, commented that "When he asked people to vote for Jack, you would have thought he was inviting them to enter the kingdom of heaven."

After Harvard, Bobby went on to the University of Virginia where he got a law degree. In 1950 he married Ethel Skakel, from another large, wealthy Catholic family, and they soon began a family of their own which eventually grew to eleven children.

Barely had Bobby completed law school and become a father than he set off with his brother and his sister Patricia for a seven week trip that took them to Israel, India, Indochina and Japan. It was Joe's idea that he should go. Jack was not at first enthusiastic about the idea, as Bobby tended to be morose. The two brothers, eight years apart in age, had not had much to do with one another, only meeting at family get togethers while they were growing up. But Joe was determined that Bobby would find his place in the family's political machine as his brother's most loyal aide and enforcer.

On his return, Bobby went to work at the Department of Justice, but took time out in 1952 to manage his brother's Senate campaign. He worked eighteen hour days, building a web of political organizations that reached every corner of Massachusetts, distinct from the local party organizations. He cleared out local politicians who were adding nothing to the campaign and built a team of some 25,000 volunteers whom he could control. His Harvard football friend Kenneth O'Donnell joined the campaign, and became one of his brother's closest political aides, accompanying him to the White House. Bobby finally won the respect from his father he had always sought, as a ruthless political operator.

Joe's next move to further Bobby's career was to call in a favor from Senator Joseph McCarthy, whose reelection he had helped finance. McCarthy was a good family friend. He had been a guest at Bobby's wedding, and half the Kennedy family had attended his wedding in 1953, at which Eunice Kennedy was a bridesmaid; Jean, the woman McCarthy married, was the closest friend of Bobby's wife Ethel.

Two years before, McCarthy had launched his demagogic campaign to rid America of communists and fellow travelers. In the new Senate he was to chair the Subcommittee on Investigations, and he agreed to take Bobby on as his assistant counsel. Jack Kennedy joined as one of four Democrats on the Subcommittee. This was an episode that would haunt the two brothers for years.

In 1957 Bobby became chief counsel of a new committee chaired by Senator John McLellan, set up to investigate corruption in the labor unions. It was known as the Rackets Committee, and again Jack Kennedy was also appointed to it. Joe was furious, believing their participation would jeopardise labor support for Jack's 1960 presidential campaign.

To a degree Joe was right, because the brothers made enemies of the Teamsters Union bosses, particularly Jimmy Hoffa. But, by having him appearing regularly on television, they were able to establish Jack as a national figure crusading against corruption. This image was enhanced when Bobby published a bestseller about the committee's campaign to break the hold of the Mafia over the unions—*The Enemy Within*.

The irony of Bobby's clash with the Mafia was that Joe had dealt with the Mob for years, first in the liquor trade during the Prohibition era, and then when he purchased the Chicago Merchandise Mart. When he failed to persuade his sons not to get involved with the Rackets Committee, there is evidence that he sought to limit the damage by making a deal with Chicago Mafia boss Sam Giancana to support Jack's 1960 run for the presidency.

Right: **Washington, D.C., March 1957**
Jack and Bobby confer during a hearing of the Senate Labor Rackets Committee on the activities of the Teamsters Union. Bobby was counsel for the committee.

Things do not happen. Things are made to happen.

Joe Kennedy

Right: **Boston, 1952**
Jack, second from right, with
Bobby and three of his sisters
working on his Senate campaign.

People say I am ruthless. I am not ruthless. And if I find the man who is calling me ruthless, I shall destroy him.

Bobby Kennedy

Right: **Boston, 1952**
Bobby, his wife Ethel, and Jack laugh over an article describing Jack's success in winning the Senate seat for Massachusetts.

A political marriage

As with most aspects of Kennedy's career, it was his father who decided it was time for him to marry. Joe came across the nominally Catholic, twenty-one year old Jacqueline Bouvier in 1950, and the following year got friends to arrange a match-making dinner party for Kennedy to meet the candidate. When Jackie didn't take the bait, another dinner was arranged in May 1952. This time it worked.

In the bourgeois marriage market of the day, Jackie had breeding but no money. Her father, John Bouvier, had made a small fortune on the stock exchange and lost it during the Depression. Her mother, Janet Lee, divorced Jackie's father for his philandering and alcoholism, and later married Hugh D. Auchincloss, a merchant banker and a Standard Oil heir. Jackie spent her teenage years in comfort, and was sent to an exclusive Connecticut girls' school.

Jackie's family claimed to be from refined stock. The Bouviers were supposedly French aristocrats; in fact, they had been artisans back home in Pont Saint Esprit in the Rhone Valley. Her mother's family, the Lees, claimed to be of Irish descent; in fact Janet's father was Jewish, and had changed his name from Levy to Lee to further his career in banking. But somehow Joe missed all this.

Jackie spent two years at Vassar College, then won a Paris *Vogue* essay competition, in which she discussed the three artists she would most like to have known—Sergei Diaghilev, Oscar Wilde and Charles Baudelaire. The prize was a year studying in Paris at the Sorbonne. When she returned to America she finished her studies at George Washington University in Washington D.C.

Jackie worked for a while as a photo-journalist at the *Times-Herald* in Washington, where Kathleen Kennedy had worked before her. She wrote a flattering piece on Kennedy when he won his

Senate seat, and was in London for the coronation of Queen Elizabeth II when Kennedy proposed marriage, by telegram.

Jackie's mother had instilled into Jackie the importance of marrying money, as her stepfather was not going to leave her any. Joe Sr. not only took a shine to Jackie from the start, but also told her that her future husband had a trust fund of $10 million, though in the event of his death it would pass to his children.

As soon as Jackie had accepted Jack's proposal, the Kennedys immediately began preparing the wedding of the year—a media event that would underpin their political ambitions for Jack. It was Joe who organized and paid for the wedding, in September 1953. The reception of over thirteen hundred guests was a political *Who's Who,* and received front page coverage in the *New York Times* and the *Washington Post.*

A Catholic politician has to have a Catholic wife ... She should have class. Jackie probably had more class than any girl we've ever seen around here.

Joe Kennedy

Next page: **Hyannis Port, Massachusetts, June 27, 1953**
A widely circulated publicity photograph of Jack and his fiancée Jackie Bouvier playing tennis.

Joe Kennedy not only condoned the marriage, he ordained it.

Lem Billings

Right: **St Mary's Church, Newport, Rhode Island, September 12, 1953**
Jack and Jackie were married in the local church where Jackie's mother and stepfather, Hughdie Auchincloss, had their vacation home.

Next page: **Jackie and Jack's wedding breakfast, September 12, 1953**
There was a reception for over 1,300 guests. They enjoyed creamed chicken and slices from a four-foot-high wedding cake, and later danced to music from the Meyer Davis Band.

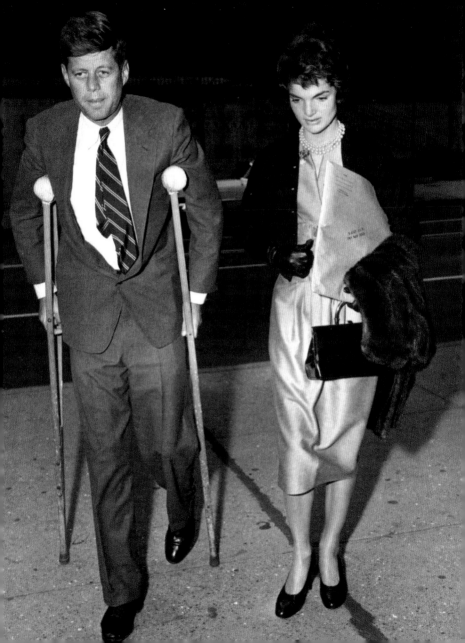

A display of courage

As a young Senator, Kennedy was frequently on crutches, and he was determined to prevent his condition degenerating further. So when the doctors at Boston's Lahey Clinic advised that his Addison's disease would make operating on his back extremely dangerous, he found a clinic in New York to take on his case.

In October 1954 he underwent an operation to break his backbone and reset it. Within three days he was in a coma, and a priest was called to administer the last rites. It took months for him to recover, and in February the last rites were said for him again.

While recuperating, Kennedy had the idea for a book about senators who had shown outstanding political courage. The book—*Profiles in Courage*—contained profiles of eight senators, but it was soon rumored that it had been ghosted by Theodore Sorensen and others. This didn't stop it becoming a major best-seller.

Joe Sr. was determined it should win a Pulitzer Prize for biography. The fact that it had not even been nominated was hardly a problem. He got onto his old friend, the journalist Arthur Krock, who was on the Pulitzer board, and had him fix it.

Kennedy undoubtedly displayed enormous physical courage throughout his life. But when the Senate turned against Senator Joe McCarthy and censured him in December 1954 with a vote of 67-22 for his anti-communist witch-hunting activities, Kennedy was one of only two Senators absent for the vote. Eleanor Roosevelt, the widow of the former president, acidly remarked that Kennedy could do with "less profile, and more courage."

Left: **New York, October 11, 1954**

Entering hospital on crutches with Jackie.

Our political life is becoming so expensive, so mechanized and so dominated by professional politicians and public relations men that the idealist who dreams of independent statesmanship is rudely awakened by the necessities of election

John F. Kennedy, *Profiles in Courage*

Right: **Book signing, 1957**

Signing copies of *Profiles in Courage*, the book which won Kennedy the Pulitzer Prize for biography—after massive lobbying by his father and Arthur Krock, the *New York Times* journalist who was on the Pulitzer board.

Winning a national profile

During his first ten years in politics Kennedy hardly made a mark on the national stage. He was responsible for no great legislation in Congress and, although profiled in up-market magazines and newspapers, most Americans had not heard of him.

All this changed after the presidential campaign of 1956. The Democrats chose Adlai Stevenson as their candidate, a man the Kennedys despised so thoroughly for his ineffectual liberalism that Bobby—whom Stevenson invited to travel the country with him during the campaign—voted for his rival, Dwight D. Eisenhower.

Kennedy, against his father's advice, decided to seek the vice presidential nomination. The Democratic Convention in August 1956 opened with the screening of a documentary entitled "The Pursuit of Happiness," which celebrated President Roosevelt's New Deal policies of the thirties. The film was narrated by Kennedy, who appeared in person when it was presented. The *New York Times* commented: "Kennedy came before the convention tonight as a movie star."

The invitation to narrate had come through Peter Lawford, a minor Hollywood star married to Kennedy's sister Patricia. Although it has never been proved, the rumor soon spread that it was Joe who financed the film.

Whereas, four years before, the convention had been seen on television in only eight million homes, in 1956 this figure rose to forty million. Demonstrators from Massachusetts holding "Kennedy for President" banners miraculously appeared in front of the cameras, even though Kennedy was actually running for vice president. Kennedy's appeal to the convention, and to the nation, was further boosted by the presence at his side throughout the week of a heavily pregnant Jackie. Meanwhile, on the convention floor Bobby worked tirelessly as a delegate canvassing support.

On the second ballot Kennedy lost by only thirty eight votes. Many southern delegates, concerned about the growing civil rights momentum, had voted for him rather than his liberal opponent, Estes Kefauver. Kennedy's gracious concession speech won wide applause within the party and established him as a credible presidential candidate for 1960. He built on this to boost his national profile by touring twenty-four states and making 150 speeches.

Amazingly, the family kept secret Kennedy's fast deteriorating health, which landed him in hospital nine times between 1955 and 1957. He had abscesses on his back, colitis and venereal infections, and had difficulty tying his shoe laces. The cocktail of drugs he took to keep him going included testosterone and Nembutal.

In the Senate, Kennedy helped his southern Democratic supporters by quietly backing wrecking amendments to the 1957 Civil Rights Act that would have given the vote to black people. He joined the Rackets Committee, where Bobby was chief counsel, to win the support of rank and file labor, whose trade unions had been hijacked by corrupt bosses often in league with organized crime.

Kennedy finally made it onto the Senate Foreign Relations Committee in 1957, and spoke in favor of Algerian independence from France. But he also argued for a more interventionist role for the U.S. in foreign affairs. When the Soviets launched the first space satellite he called for more military spending to close the "missile gap." Even at that time, Kennedy must have known that the "missile gap" was vastly in favor of the U.S.

UTAH
UTAH
MICHIGAN
MASSACHUSETTS
1956
EMOCRATIC
NATIONAL
CONVENTION

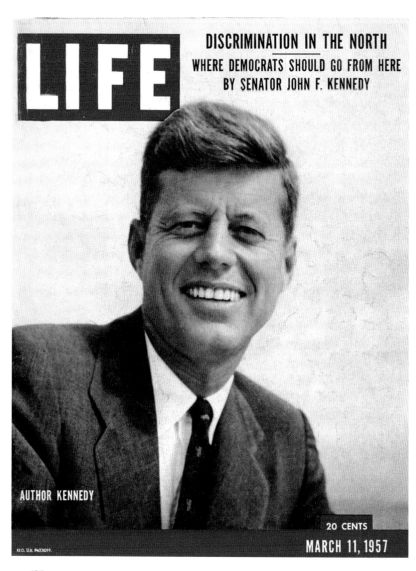

LIFE

DISCRIMINATION IN THE NORTH

WHERE DEMOCRATS SHOULD GO FROM HERE
BY SENATOR JOHN F. KENNEDY

AUTHOR KENNEDY

20 CENTS

MARCH 11, 1957

REG. U.S. PAT.OFF.

In 1960 the Democrats will (it now appears) be matched against a tough, skillful, shrewd opponent in Richard M. Nixon.

Previous page: **National Democratic Convention, Chicago, August 1956**
Kennedy with Senator Estes Kefauver on his right and Presidential candidate Adlai Stevenson on his left.

Left: ***LIFE*** **magazine cover, March 11, 1957**
After the 1957 presidential campaign Kennedy had gained national fame.

I don't want my young children to be brought up by nurses and Secret Service men.

Jackie Kennedy

Left: **Washington D.C., March 25, 1958**
With baby daughter Caroline at four months.

The 1958 Senate election—a breeze

Now that Kennedy was a celebrity, he just needed a landslide win in the 1958 Senate elections to position him for his assault on the presidency. His opponent, Vincent J. Celeste, was largely unknown, which made it even more vital to make a stir and bring out the vote.

Teddy, the youngest of the family, was nominally in charge of the campaign, but he had a much less ruthess style of leadership from that exercised by Bobby six years previously. Joe, as always, was in the background, but less of a presence than before. The real drive came from the team which had come together around Kennedy over the years, led by Kenneth O'Donnell, Larry O'Brien, Dave Powers and Ted Sorensen. No less a supporter than Cardinal Cushing lent a hand, by having a statement read out at every mass in the Boston archdiocese one Sunday reminding all Catholics to register to vote.

But it was Kennedy himself who controlled the details, making sure that each group and each community was targeted. Over the summer he visited half the towns and cities of Massachusetts, and then took off across the country giving speeches on behalf of other Democrats. Throughout he had his eye on burnishing a public image that would carry him through to the presidency.

His victory was unprecedented in Massachusetts history, and was the largest by far of any in the Senate that year. Kennedy won by a massive 874,608 votes, 73.6% of all votes cast.

Right: **Washington, D.C., April 21, 1958**
Kennedy in his Senate office.

The race for the presidency

Kennedy faced four main rivals for the Democratic nomination in 1960: Adlai Stevenson, the liberals' hero; Senator Stuart Symington, a former Airforce Secretary; Lyndon B. Johnson, the Senate Majority Leader and a powerful political fixer; and Senator Hubert Humphrey. But from the start the man to beat was Humphrey.

The challenge for Kennedy was to retain the support of the segregationist southern Democrats while appeasing the liberals in the party, and then, the nomination won, to prove he was as reliable in defense of U.S. interests as the Eisenhower administration. Careful choreography was required, using all the public relations techniques of the new age of mass consumption and television.

Kennedy had many advantages. He had a well tested campaign team with a formidable database on each state, listed on some fifty thousand file cards. There was plenty of cash to grease the palms of local politicians, print literature, secure press and television coverage, or buy sodas for outdoor crowds. Kennedy himself flew everywhere in his private plane, the *Caroline*, the only candidate with this advantage. He assembled an Academic Advisory Group of leading young academics to give gravitas to his pronouncements, even if he mostly ignored their analysis.

The first test was the Wisconsin primary, where the strength of the labor unions made Humphrey confident he could win. But Kennedy found that his work on the Senate Rackets Committee had won him support and neutralized Humphrey's appeal.

Right: **LIFE cover, April 21, 1958**
Family group with baby Caroline, taken at their Georgetown home.

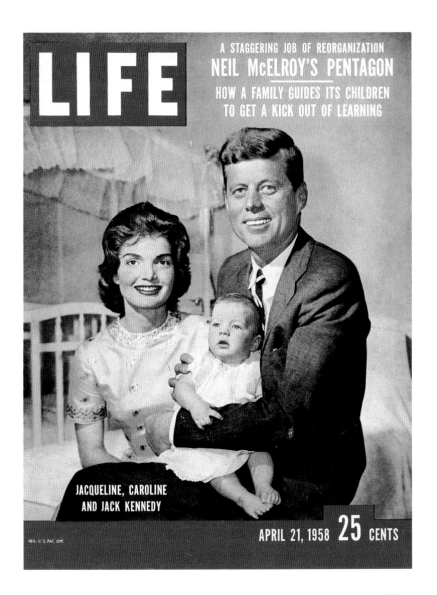

LI FE

A STAGGERING JOB OF REORGANIZATION
NEIL McELROY'S PENTAGON

HOW A FAMILY GUIDES ITS CHILDREN
TO GET A KICK OUT OF LEARNING

JACQUELINE, CAROLINE
AND JACK KENNEDY

REG. U. S. PAT. OFF.

APRIL 21, 1958 **25** CENTS

KENNEDY
FOR PRESIDENT

LEADERSHIP FOR THE 60's

Bobby helped get the Catholic vote out by the unconventional means of covertly distributing anti-Catholic literature to Catholic households.

Kennedy won with 56 percent of the vote, but did badly in Protestant areas. Humphrey had made Kennedy's religion an issue from the start and the local press and television took the cue. As the votes were being counted, the young CBS television anchor Walter Cronkite asked Kennedy how the Catholic vote was holding up. Kennedy was furious and threatened that he would not give another interview unless they dropped that line of questioning.

Against the advice of his father, Kennedy decided to challenge Humphrey in West Virginia, one of the poorest states, with a large working class, high unemployment—and an electorate that was 95% Protestant. He tackled the Catholic issue head-on, telling an audience: "I refuse to believe that I was denied the right to be president on the day I was baptized."

Jackie was brought in as an exotic attraction, not campaigning so much as presenting herself for viewing. Local people stared at her in her haute couture as if she had arrived from another planet.

Kennedy won West Virginia by a margin of 61 to 39 percent. But his victory had less to do with political campaigning and more to do with the cases of banknotes that were judiciously distributed around the state. Democratic Party bosses were encouraged to put Kennedy's name forward as the "approved candidate" on their local "slate." The story goes that one lucky boss, who had already received $2,000 from Humphrey, received another $35,000 from the Kennedy camp, when he had only asked for one-tenth of that.

Left: **Election poster, 1960**
Designed for the Presidential campaign by Donald Wilson.

Whereas Humphrey's official spending on his campaign was no more than $25,000, Kennedy's was $274,000. But it is widely believed that the real figure was much higher than this, with some estimates as high as $5 million. There had never before been spending on this scale in an American election.

Johnson kept out of the primaries, and didn't declare his candidacy until a few days before the July Democratic Convention, by which time Kennedy virtually had the election sewn up. Johnson's approach was to disparage his rival for his youth and poor health, leaking information to the press about Kennedy's Addison's disease, and raising once again his religion and his father's pro-Nazi sympathies. But the Kennedy machine was able to squash these attacks before they got mileage in the press.

One of the great mysteries of the campaign is how Kennedy came to invite Johnson to run as the Democratic candidate for vice president. The two men loathed one another, and Bobby's hatred of Johnson was visceral. The official Kennedy story is that Joe decided to have Johnson on the ticket because he would help carry Texas. But Kennedy was likely to carry Texas anyway, whereas in the event he lost California, which he would most likely have won if he had stuck with his original choice of Stuart Symington.

One story has it that Chicago Mafia boss Sam Giancana called in a favor with Joe Kennedy, though quite why he would have been so keen to have Johnson as vice president is not clear. A more likely explanation is that Johnson blackmailed Kennedy, perhaps by threatening to reveal secrets about his private life. This version gains plausibility in view of Johnson's close friendship with FBI director

Right: **Mullens, West Virginia, April 1960**
Campaigning for the miners' vote.

J. Edgar Hoover, who had a thick file on Kennedy.

The only notable thing about Kennedy's acceptance speech at the convention was his new clarion call: "But I tell you the New Frontier is here whether we seek it or not." Quite what this New Frontier represented was left to the imagination of the audience.

In the ensuing campaign against Richard Nixon, Kennedy drew the sting from the religious issue when he told a meeting of three hundred Protestant ministers in Houston that if faced with a conflict between church and state as president, he would resign his office. His comments were broadcast again and again by television stations across America.

As in his previous campaigns, Kennedy set out to appeal to each segment of the electorate. Winning the support of female voters was the easy part. Winning the black vote was more tricky if he was not to upset southern Democrats. But as the election drew near luck intervened. Nixon had refused to intervene to get the black civil rights leader Martin Luther King Jr. out of jail. But Kennedy decided to help behind the scenes, and then called King's wife Coretta. On the last Sunday before the election the Kennedy campaign distributed literally millions of leaflets outside southern baptist churches telling of Kennedy's action. The story was missed by the local and national press.

On the day Kennedy beat Nixon by less than 120,000 votes, the closest election since 1884. Even with the vast funds at his disposal, Kennedy barely scraped home.

Left: **Texas, September 1960**
Kennedy with his vice-presidential running mate, Lyndon B. Johnson. Bound together by a collision of political ambitions, the two men hated each other. Johnson referred to Kennedy as "that spavined hunchback."

Winning the women's vote

Kennedy first learnt the importance of getting out the women's vote when he won his Senate seat in 1952. Then, his courtship of the women of Massachusetts was inspired and direct, playing on his sex appeal, his youth and his vulnerability. No politician before him had made quite this impact.

The central weapon of the Kennedy team in attracting women voters was amazingly simple: it was the tea party. In all, some 75,000 women attended these events in the course of the campaign. They were organized by Pauline "Polly" Fitzgerald, a first cousin of Rose Kennedy, and Helen Keyes, a local gym teacher, and they were attended by women from diverse backgrounds.

Kennedy's hands were often scratched by long fingernails of women desperate for a touch, women who dissolved into tears if he gave them a full handshake. At day's end, the candidate often had to soak his abrasions in hot water and apply balm. His cuffs were ripped off and his shirt sleeves so frequently shredded that staff members carried replacements.

Hugh Sidey, journalist and friend

Left: **On the election campaign trail, 1960.**
Adoring women flock to touch Kennedy's outstretched hand.

In each town the organizers would recruit a locally popular Kennedy supporter, usually a male professional, to help organize the event. Fitzgerald recalled: "The man we'd get from each community would form a committee of 50 women who were prominent for one reason or another, and we'd ask each of the 50 women to get in touch with 10 people to see if they would come to the tea and then ask each of those 10 people if they could think of 10 more; in the end, you'd have 5,000 people."

Engraved invitations were mailed. For some recipients, explained Kennedy aide Dave Powers, "the only thing they ever find in the mailbox is a bill, and they find this invitation to go to a reception at a hotel and meet Rose Kennedy and the rest of them—they'd put on their best hat and coat and be there."

The *Berkshire Eagle* noted of a tea party in Lenox, attended by more than 2,000 women, that it "was the greatest women's political rally ever staged in the area since women were given the voting franchise more than 30 years ago." In every sense, the paper concluded, the tea party was a success. "The Kennedys, who footed the bill, were satisfied; the women, most of whom were bedecked in Sunday's finest, enjoyed themselves; and several milliners and dress shop operators of the county, who were in attendance, were more than satisfied because [the tea] was responsible for an unusual end-of-the-summer run on hats, frocks, and shoes."

Most of the teas were held in large rented halls or elegant hotel ballrooms. With his mother and sisters at his side, Kennedy usually began by thanking everyone for coming, while expressing the hope that they would support his candidacy in November. He and his family would then form a reception line and greet every person in attendance. Later, the guests would receive in the mail a note from the candidate thanking them for their support.

The *New York Times* observed: "Unmarried, wealthy, Harvardishly casual in his dress, and with a distinguished war record in addition to his other attainments, he just about bracketed the full range of emotional interests of such an all-feminine group—maternal at one end and romantic at the other."

The *Boston American* reported on election day, "there was evidence that women for the first time were taking complete advantage of their political emancipation … They were turning out en masse, with babes in arms, in many cases."

These tea parties … appear to have many women, of all ages, quite excited about the young candidate. They ooh and they aah when you mention him, they tell you they think he is wonderful, they give every indication of yearning to run their fingers through his tousled hair. They never mention any qualifications that he may have or may lack for service in the Senate, but this would be too much to expect.

Haverhill Gazette, October 5, 1952

A NEW LEADER FOR THE 60's

KENNEDY FOR PRESIDENT

"...give me your voice, your hand, your vote" for a strong PRESIDENT VOTE FOR KENNEDY

Democratic National Committee
1001 Connecticut Avenue, N.W. Washington, D.C.

KENNEDY
JOHNSON

DEMOCRATIC NATIONAL COMMITTEE, 1001 CONNECTICUT AVENUE, N.W. WASHINGTON, D.C.

YOUR
FIRST
VOTE

PENN.

THE DEMOCRATS
CARE ABOUT
TOMORROW

Kennedy: Leader for the 60's

We love you on TV. You're better than Elvis Presley ...

students at Louisville, Kentucky

Previous page: **Campaign materials, 1960**

Left: **At the Democratic Convention, Los Angeles, July 1960**
Surrounded by supporters.

Next page: **Los Angeles Airport, July 1960.**
A welcoming committee of supporters dancing in a conga line.

Dangerous connections

American politics is a brutal game, and both presidential contenders were going for broke.

For his part Nixon was convinced that his victory would be secure if the Eisenhower administration could succeed in eliminating Fidel Castro before the election. The CIA was preparing an invasion force of Cuban émigrés in Guatemala, but to be sure of success the experts were convinced that Castro should first be assassinated. Sam Giancana, the ruthless head of the Chicago Mafia syndicate, was entrusted to organize the hit, which he insisted must be by poisoning, as marksmen would have little chance of escape. He hired the notorious Los Angeles Mafia hitman John Rosselli to do the job.

At the same time as Giancana was being hired by the Nixon camp, he was in negotiation with Joe Kennedy. Joe was the mastermind of his son's campaign strategy, and he was preparing backup plans for every marginal state. Illinois, with twenty-seven of the 537 electoral college votes, could go either way, and Joe needed some extra help.

When the election votes were counted, Kennedy won Illinois by the narrow margin of 9,400 votes. Yet in the state capital of Chicago, his majority was a massive 456,312. The Republicans cried foul, and immediately accused Mayor Richard Daley of rigging the vote. This may well have been the case, though nothing was ever proved. Either way, it does not rule out there having been an additional contribution from Sam Giancana.

What Giancana most had to offer was manpower. In 1960 the mob dominated all the major unions in Chicago, more than a hundred in all. Giancana could ensure a high labor turnout for the vote, and he could also put drivers in every precinct. His support was all the more important since Teamster Union boss Jimmy Hoffa was enraged at the Kennedy brothers for going after him in the Senate Rackets Committee hearings on labor union corruption, and would be doing everything he could to stop Kennedy.

It seems that Joe did not know Giancana personally, though in his liquor business and as owner of the Chicago Merchandise Mart he undoubtedly rubbed shoulders with the criminal underworld. The Mafia had close links with the entertainment business, as did both Giancana and Joe, and his daughter Patricia was married to the actor Peter Lawford, a prominent member of Frank Sinatra's Rat Pack. Sinatra considered himself the entertainment world's ambassador to the world of organized crime.

It is claimed that Joe had his first meeting with Giancana in a judge's chambers in Chicago. Subsequent meetings were arranged on golf courses and other neutral places through Sinatra, according to Sinatra's daughter Tina.

No one has revealed what Giancana expected to gain from backing Kennedy, but the most obvious benefit would have been for his syndicate to be left alone once Jack Kennedy became president, and Bobby the Attorney General. If so, he must have been furious when Bobby resumed his campaign against organized crime from the White House.

Just in case they encountered accusations later that the Kennedys had rigged the election, Joe had a plan already in place. For several years he had been cultivating F.B.I. boss J. Edgar Hoover and stroking his massive ego. Hoover was nearing retirement age and anxious to be reconfirmed in his job. With Jack president, that could be taken care of, and between them Hoover and Bobby could head off all efforts to prove election fraud.

Sinatra has had a long and wide association with hoodlums and racketeers, which seems to be continuing.

Justice Report

Right: **Kennedy campaign event, 1960**
Frank Sinatra campaigning with Jack's sister Patricia Kennedy Lawford.

The TV debates

Richard Nixon was a devious political operator, but in John F. Kennedy he met his match. The two men, just four years apart in age, were both elected to the House of Representatives in 1946. But from then on, Nixon's career raced ahead. In 1952 he was elected to the Senate, and was almost immediately elevated to be Eisenhower's vice-presidential running mate.

So when he was pitted against Kennedy for the presidency in 1960, Nixon already had eight years' experience in the White House. He struck many Americans as brusque and underhand, but won respect for standing up to a stone-throwing crowd in Caracas in 1958 and debating Khrushchev in Moscow in 1959.

The problem for Kennedy was not only to overcome charges of inexperience, but to present policies and an approach that was different from Nixon and the popular Eisenhower administration. It was hard to charge the man who had commanded U.S. forces in World War II or his vice-president as soft on communism, abroad or at home. The 1950s saw the U.S. fighting a bloody war in Korea, and at home supporting the McCarthy anti-communist purges.

In the late fifties opinion polls consistently showed the American public concerned about Soviet Russia and, after 1959, about Cuba too. Kennedy's response, beginning with a speech to the Senate in August 1958, was to warn that there was a "missile gap." Russian superiority in Inter-Continental and Intermediate-Range Ballistic Missiles meant that it could "destroy 85 percent of our industry, 43 of our 50 largest cities, and most of the nation's population." This was out and out scare-mongering, and Eisenhower asked the CIA to brief Kennedy on the true situation, which was undoubtedly in America's favor. But nothing would persuade Kennedy from exploiting the fears of ordinary citizens.

Kennedy tried hard to present the Eisenhower administration as unable to generate prosperity at home, and promoted the slogan "Let's Get the Country Moving Again." In fact, despite two recessions, the economy had grown by 2.4 percent a year under Eisenhower. It was true that the economies of western Europe, Japan and the Soviet Union were expanding faster, but they were still recovering from the destruction of the war years which the U.S. had not had to suffer. Nor was it the case that Kennedy was offering a radically different approach to the economy.

The presidential campaign therefore largely came down to presentation and image. When the Kennedy side challenged Nixon to an unprecedented four live television debates, confident that their man would shine on the little screen, Eisenhower advised Nixon not to accept. But Nixon was sure he could out-debate Kennedy.

In the first debate, Nixon looked tired and uncomfortable, his stubble showing through his Lazy Shave and sweat pouring off him. Kennedy by contrast, apparently aided by methedrine shots and the delivery of a call girl to his room before the debate, looked the picture of health. Instead of scoring debating points like Nixon, he addressed the nation face on as if he already were president, and concentrated on "sound bites." In the reaction shots Kennedy looked amused or a little bored by Nixon, whereas Nixon glowered.

Polls showed that those that heard the debate on the radio thought that Nixon was the victor, his voice deeper and more authoritative. But seventy million watched on television, and among these viewers a slight majority gave the contest to Kennedy.

Next page: **Kennedy-Nixon television debate, September 26, 1960**
A family watching the debate at home.

The next three debates consolidated Kennedy's advantage. In the third debate he claimed that Nixon had "never really protested the communists seizing Cuba." Since April Nixon had been closely involved in CIA plans for a Cuban émigré invasion of Cuba to oust Castro. But it seems that CIA director Allen Dulles and his deputy, Richard Bissell, decided to break ranks and let Kennedy in on the secret to aid his election campaign. In July they arranged a meeting for Kennedy with Manuel Artime and three other Cuban émigré leaders involved in planning the invasion, and in October John Patterson, the Governor of Alabama, secretly briefed Kennedy that the Alabama National Guard was training the Cuban invasion force in Guatemala. Through the fall of 1960 Kennedy spoke several times of the need to unleash the Cuban "freedom fighters."

When, in the fourth debate, Kennedy charged Nixon with doing nothing to help the Cubans regain their country—knowing full well that Nixon was doing everything he could to that end—Nixon's hands were tied by his role in the government and he could not defend himself. His reply to Kennedy was that the U.S. could never get involved in invasion plans because that was proscribed by international law, and it would moreover encourage the Russians to become involved in Latin America. Later Nixon wrote that "for the first and only time in the campaign, I got mad at Kennedy personally." He called the Kennedy team "the most ruthless group of political operators ever mobilized for a political campaign." Coming from Nixon, that was quite a compliment.

Right: **Presidential television debate, September 26, 1960**
Kennedy and Nixon greet each other in the studio at the end of the debate.

My wife and I look forward to a new administration and a new baby.

Left: **Hyannis Port, Cape Cod, November 9, 1960**
Jack and Jackie with baby Caroline on election day.

… a dark-haired mite …

Maud Shaw, the Kennedy's nanny, on the new baby

Right: **Georgetown, Washington D.C., December 1960**
Arriving home from hospital with new baby John.

chapter 3

The White House Years

A dazzling inauguration

The Kennedy success owed much to presentation. Jack had grown up close to the world of Hollywood, and courting the media came naturally. Having won the presidency by a whisker, he seized on the Inauguration as a golden opportunity to extend his appeal.

Kennedy's inaugural speech was barely half the length of those of most of his predecessors. He took Abraham Lincoln's Gettysburg Address as the model to emulate, in its succinctness, and its call to civic duty and shared national values. Working with Theodore Sorensen, Kennedy focused on foreign affairs. The struggle for civil rights was ignored, though the African-American contralto Marian Anderson was invited to sing *The Star Spangled Banner* afterward.

Kennedy declaimed his speech with heroic deliberation, and clearly hit his mark. Polls showed that his approval rating shot up to nearly seventy-five percent. Watching on television from the Mayo Clinic, Nobel laureate Ernest Hemingway caught the mood: "Watching on the screen I was sure our President would stand any of the heat to come as he had taken the cold of that day."

"The cold of that day" referred to the sub-zero temperature in Washington. Having decreed top hats for all male dignitaries, Kennedy went bareheaded and coatless while taking the oath, giving his address, and throughout the three-and-a-half-hour parade. He appeared young, fit, and bronzed. At forty-three he was the youngest U.S. president eve to win office, with an elegant wife of thirty-one and two young children. The First Couple projected a vision of hope, in which America was a force for good.

The pre-inaugural ball had been pure Hollywood—Frank Sinatra, Gene Kelly, Nat King Cole amongst others. On the day itself, Kennedy brought the intellectuals into the political fold for the first time. Robert Frost, at eighty-six years old, was invited to read a new poem but, blinded by the bright sun, he ended up reciting "The Gift Outright." W. H. Auden, Robert Lowell, Paul Tillich, and some fifty other writers and artists were present. John Steinbeck commented: "What a joy that literacy is not *prima facie* evidence of treason."

Previous page: **Kennedy and his wife Jackie, the White House, Washington D.C., May 11, 1962**

A State dinner was held for the French Cultural Minister André Malraux at the White House on May 11, 1962. Jackie had charmed Malraux when she and Jack had visited Paris in May the previous year. Malraux had just lost his son in a car accident, but he nevertheless escorted Jackie everywhere, and agreed to arrange the loan of Leonardo da Vinci's *Mona Lisa* from the Paris Louvre Museum to the National Gallery in Washington—an unprecedented coup for Jackie. Malraux had been a successful novelist, adventurer, and left-wing activist before the Second World War, then joined the French political establishment at President de Gaulle's invitation. Jackie was in awe of him, and inviting him to the White House was a dream come true.

Next page: **The White House, Washington D.C., January 20, 1961**

The oath was administered to Kennedy by Earl Warren, Chief Justice of the Supreme Court. It was a bright, bitterly cold day, with deep snow on the ground, but Kennedy nevertheless spoke without hat or coat. Less than three years later, it was Earl Warren who was appointed to head the commission that investigated the causes of Kennedy's assassination.

And so, my fellow Americans: ask not what your country can do for you—ask what you can do for your country.

Right: **A commemorative card featuring the most famous words from Kennedy's inaugural speech, January 20, 1961**

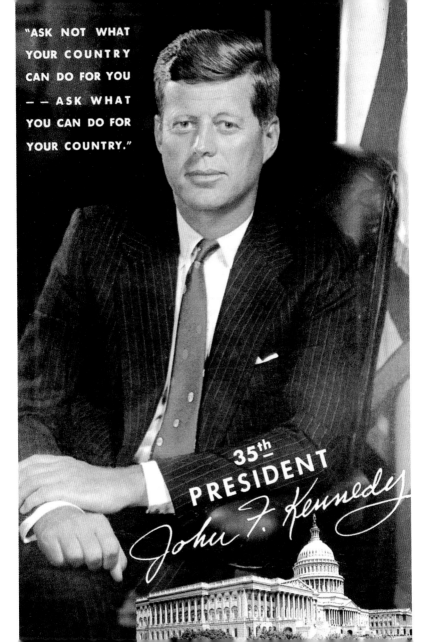

"ASK NOT WHAT YOUR COUNTRY CAN DO FOR YOU − − ASK WHAT YOU CAN DO FOR YOUR COUNTRY."

35th PRESIDENT

John F. Kennedy

The master orator

Like his political hero Winston Churchill, Kennedy became a spell-binding speechmaker. His confident presentational style charmed, inspired, and disarmed his audiences, exactly as he intended. And, just as Churchill did, he employed a deliberate technique of rhetoric formally known as *chiasmus,* a Greek word meaning a "criss-cross" arrangement of terms. Put simply, the trick is to reverse the order of two parallel clauses. The most famous example of this in action was used in Kennedy's inaugural address: "Ask not what your country can do for you—ask what you can do for your country."

Riveting stuff indeed—but the "ask not" sentiment was not Kennedy's own. There are several earlier examples of this phraseology—Warren G. Harding used it, as did Oliver Wendell Holmes Jr., in his address to the Grand Army of the Republic, May 30, 1884: " … It is now the moment when by common consent we pause to become conscious of our national life and rejoice in it; to recall what our country has done for each of us, and to ask ourselves what we can do for our country in return." Just as importantly LeBaron Russell Briggs, a turn-of-the-century Harvard professor urged students to think of their Alma Mater and: "Always ask, not 'What can she do for me?' but 'What can I do for her?'"

As a Harvard man, Kennedy would have been more than familiar with these speeches. Moreover he, or one of his speech-writers, had no doubt come across the same theme in the 1959 Walt Disney movie *Zorro: Invitation to Death*, which contained the dialogue: "Is this the time to ask what have you done for us? We should be asking what can we do for you."

It is evident that Kennedy enjoyed using the technique as much as he reveled in the applause it generated. The device was

Above: **Kennedy and Theodore Sorensen check a speech, December, 1960**

frequently a vehicle for his characteristically sardonic humor, as shown in his comment that "Washington is a city of southern efficiency and northern charm."

He had chosen a group of talented speechwriters that included Theodore Sorensen and Arthur Schlesinger Jr. True to form, Sorensen upheld the polite convention that the President wrote his own speeches, and claimed that, apart from set occasions like the State of the Union or the Democratic Convention, Kennedy usually ad-libbed entire speeches. "I'm proud of the role that I played in many of his speeches, but President Kennedy authored all of them."

Later, Sorensen took some ribbing about this. In his political column, William F. Buckley urged Americans to squarely face the world Communist revolution, or suffer the consequences. In a teasing parody of Kennedy he wrote: "Unless we learn how to cope with it, it will—as Theodore Sorensen would put it—cope with us."

The United States must be so strong that no enemy or coalition of enemies can attack us without the certain knowledge that they will be destroyed by our retaliatory forces.

St. Louis Globe-Democrat, January 15th, 1961

Right: **Front cover of *This Week* magazine, the supplement to the *St Louis Globe Democrat,* January 15, 1961**

Kennedy could not have anticipated the scale of the crises he was about to confront.

Next page: **Rehearsal for the Inaugural Gala, National Guard Armory, January 19, 1961**

Nat King Cole is standing at the microphone. Frank Sinatra (third from left) produced and directed the gala. Others present in the photograph include Jimmy Durante, Ella Fitzgerald, and Harry Belafonte.

January 15, 1961

This Week
MAGAZINE

St. Louis Globe-Democrat.

"The next year, the next decade, in all likelihood the next generation, will require more bravery and wisdom on our part than any period in our history." —JOHN F. KENNEDY

THE NEW PRESIDENT ANSWERS 10 MAJOR QUESTIONS...PAGE 6

Let the word go forth from this time and place, to friend and foe alike, that the torch has been passed to a new generation of Americans—born in this century, tempered by war, proud of our ancient heritage—and unwilling to witness or permit the slow undoing of those human rights to which this nation has always been committed.

Right: **Presidential Box at the Inaugural Ball, January 20, 1961**
There were five inaugural balls. Jack attended all five, but Jackie lasted through just three.

The immediate political challenges

Kennedy's presidency was, above all, about foreign affairs. This was not simply because he had little personal interest in most domestic social and economic issues, and had been trained from youth as an expert in foreign affairs. Nor was it just because his administration was beset by foreign crises from the word go. Both factors played their part, but the more fundamental reason derived from the international situation the United States faced in the early sixties.

America had emerged from World War II as the unchallenged imperial power, dominating the world economy, and with its allies as well as its enemies reduced to destitution. It had overseen the reconstruction of Western Europe through the economic program of Marshall Aid, a program that involved an unprecedented transfer of financial resources from the United States to Europe.

In eleven weeks I went from senator to president, and in that short space of time I inherited Laos, Cuba, Berlin, the nuclear threat, and all the rest.

Right: **The Oval Office, the White House, March 17, 1961**
Kennedy works at his desk in his customary standing position, to ease the pain in his back which is encased in a back brace. His personal secretary, Evelyn Lincoln, looks on.

In South East Asia the U.S. had rebuilt the regional economy not only through financial aid, but by re-engineering Japanese society from top to bottom and appointing Japan as its gatekeeper to oversee the lesser regional powers.

By the time Kennedy was elected president, however, Europe and Japan had recovered sufficiently to become economic and political competitors. Throughout the fifties the economic growth rates of these two regions consistently surpassed those of the United States.

The nations which later came to be collectively known as the Third World contained many of the resources that U.S. industry required—especially raw materials and agricultural products—and some were also markets with significant potential. Several of these nations had already achieved political independence from European imperialist powers, while many others were in the last stages of liberation wars. All were beginning to assert their own interests, and it was U.S. policy to guide them into its sphere of influence through a combination of "hard" military power and economic and cultural influence, "soft" power.

American capitalists aimed to break down all geographical and social barriers to expand their markets, and when Kennedy won the presidency the U.S. was still smarting from the loss of China to the world marketplace. There was concern that the Soviet Union and China, through example as much as direct intervention, might help other nations to develop independently from the U.S.-dominated world system. This concern was at the heart of the "Cold War", a war which, as U.S. policy makers early recognized, would necessarily erupt into hot wars. In fact the U.S. military actively contemplated a pre-emptive nuclear strike to remove the Soviet Union as a political competitor, and this option was weighed by

Kennedy as a way of pushing the Russians out of Europe.

Three Cold War regional flashpoints were already on the agenda when Kennedy took office. In Indochina, the U.S. puppet government of Ngo Dinh Diem in South Vietnam was reeling under the nationalist assault from the north led by Ho Chi Minh. Eisenhower had resisted direct intervention after the defeat of the French colonial army in 1954, but much greater involvement would be necessary to halt the "red tide"

Berlin was another area of acute conflict. After Hitler's defeat the Soviet army advanced as far as Berlin, and in the subsequent peace negotiations the city was divided into four zones controlled by Soviet, U.S., British, and French forces. The subsequent flow of German citizens from the east to the west led to constant tensions.

Ironically, the place where Cold War tensions became most acute was a Caribbean island of six million people only ninety miles from U.S. shores. Latin America had been firmly within the U.S. sphere of influence for more than a century, but the region looked suddenly less compliant when, on January 1, 1959, a nationalist revolution triumphed in Cuba, under the leadership of Fidel Castro. The overthrow of Castro soon became a U.S. policy obsession.

At home a powerful civil rights movement to end discrimination against Afro-Americans had been gaining ground since the early fifties and had support among liberal sections of the Democratic Party. Kennedy had ignored it as far as he could during his campaign for the presidency and, wrongly as things turned out, did not envisage that it would be center stage during his first term.

As for the economy, Kennedy intended to leave it to those who knew about such things to ensure that it continued to deliver prosperity to the American consumer and a second term in office for him as president.

Cuba—the ticking bomb

After winning independence from Spain in 1898, Cuba fell into the arms of the United States and became effectively its colony. Over the next sixty years it was ruled by a succession of U.S.-sponsored regimes, and the great majority of the population languished in poverty and backwardness. By the fifties the United States was protecting the corrupt and brutal regime of President Fulgencio Batista, which was in bed with the Mafia. Havana had become the gambling, drugs and prostitution capital of the western world.

Kennedy knew this world well. He had visited the fleshpots of Havana in 1957 and 1958, where he met with Batista, stayed with Ambassador Earl Smith—a strong Batista supporter—and was reportedly compromised by the Mafia. A former lawyer for the mob has claimed that Kennedy accepted the hospitality of gambling mobster Santo Trafficante, who supplied three prostitutes for Kennedy in the Hotel Comodoro and watched the action through a two-way mirror.

The Cuban Revolution of January 1, 1959, was enormously popular in Cuba, and was supported by liberals in the United States too. The new government led by Fidel Castro immediately set about establishing literacy programs, providing education and health care for all, and redistributing land to landless peasants.

The U.S. extended diplomatic recognition to the new government within a week, but only two months later the U.S. National Security Council met in secret to discuss plans for installing a new government. In public the U.S. administration claimed to support Cuban agrarian reform, but all the time it was giving asylum to torturers from the former Batista regime, and supporting sabotage operations against the island.

The Cuban Revolution was never going to be accepted by the United States, not because it was "communist," but because it threatened U.S. interests and set an unwelcome example to the rest of the region. Relations between the two countries deteriorated rapidly. The Cuban government confiscated more than a million acres of land from three U.S. companies, including United Fruit. When Cuba made a trade agreement with the Soviet Union, the U.S.-owned oil refineries in Cuba refused to refine Soviet crude oil. Cuba seized the refineries, the U.S. ended the quota arrangement for Cuban sugar imports, and the Soviet Union responded by agreeing to purchase the 700,000 tonnes of sugar that would normally have gone to the U.S.

Cuba became an issue for Kennedy even before he became president, and remained an obsession throughout his presidency. He was aware early on through a tip-off that the Eisenhower administration was training Cuban émigrés to invade Cuba, and used the information to good effect in outflanking Richard Nixon in their final television debate in October, 1960. Nixon, bound by secrecy as a member of the administration, attacked Kennedy's advocacy of an invasion as contravening international law.

In the days following Kennedy's inauguration the CIA, which was by now considering committing U.S. troops as well as Cuban émigrés, began urging Kennedy to prepare for an invasion of Cuba. But the State Department was concerned that, if the U.S. were seen to be openly involved, there could be uprisings throughout Latin America. Kennedy shared this concern, and asked for plans which would not involve direct U.S. intervention. The Cuban exiles, the CIA, and the Pentagon complied, assuming that if success were in doubt Kennedy would have to commit U.S. forces. Meanwhile, the CIA contracted Mafia boss John Rosselli to assassinate Castro.

The Bay of Pigs invasion—defeat and revenge

The invasion of Cuba was finally set in motion on April 15, 1961 when eight B-26 bombers, piloted by U.S.-trained Cuban exiles, attacked Cuban air bases, but succeeded in destroying only five of Cuba's forty combat aircraft. Two days later the invasion force of 1,400 men landed at the Bay of Pigs on the south coast, but the Cuban armed forces were soon in place to confront them. Richard Bissell, Deputy Director of the CIA, authorized six U.S. pilots in three B-26 bombers to launch a napalm attack, but two of the planes were shot down. Cuba found identifying documents and denounced U.S. involvement at the United Nations.

Within three days the invasion was defeated, with 114 Cuban exiles killed and 1,189 captured. Kennedy had suffered the first serious defeat of his political career. In order to get the exiles released 18 months later he had to hand over to Castro $3 million in cash plus $50 million in tractors, medical supplies, and baby food.

Kennedy was shattered by the defeat. He issued a statement assuming full responsibility for the fiasco, in which he said that "victory has a hundred fathers and defeat is an orphan," and he told the press "I'm the responsible officer of the government." But he was furious with himself for having relied unquestioningly on the expertise of the CIA and the Pentagon. He fired CIA director Allen Dulles and his deputy, Richard Bissell.

Right: **Cover of *LIFE* magazine, May 10, 1963**
Two years after the failed invasion of Cuba at the Bay of Pigs, fury at Kennedy for having failed to provide air cover was still strong, and there was a clamor for an all-out invasion that would get rid of Fidel Castro for good.

LIFE

**RAW UNTOLD TRUTH
BY MEN WHO FOUGHT**

Bay of Pigs

**Heartbreaking Price
They Paid for
U.S. Miscalculations**

MAY 10 · 1963 · 25¢

185

Kennedy had been reared by his father never to contemplate defeat. He resolved to get even with Castro, and within two days he set up a task force under General Maxwell Taylor to study the lessons of the fiasco. He then appointed General Edward Lansdale—a man with long experience of counter-insurgency in the Philippines and South Vietnam—to develop a new plan for overthrowing Castro.

In November 1961 Kennedy put Lansdale in operational charge of this program, code named Operation Mongoose, with Robert Kennedy leading an interagency group to oversee it. Bobby told the CIA that Cuba was "the top priority in the U.S. Government—all else is secondary."

Over the next eleven months various schemes were discussed to provide an excuse for direct U.S. military intervention if an internal popular uprising failed to materialize. These included blowing up a U.S. ship at the Guantánamo naval base and shooting down a drone aircraft, claiming it was carrying college students.

Left and next page: **Orange Bowl Stadium, Miami, December 29, 1962**
At a ceremony for surviving members of Brigade 2506, the Cuban émigré force defeated at the Bay of Pigs, Kennedy receives the brigade flag from commander Pepe San Román. The flag had been hidden by a member of the brigade during his time in a Cuban jail. Jackie said a few words in Spanish, and Jack announced that the Cubans would return to "a free Cuba." The stadium erupted with chants of "Guerra! Guerra!"

Operation Mongoose

Operation Mongoose set out a carefully choreographed terror campaign culminating in U.S. military intervention in Cuba in October 1962—the month of the Cuban missile crisis. Lansdale's proposal was to infiltrate the island, create political cells, and organize sabotage and subversion. Mobster John Rosselli was again enlisted to organize the murder of Castro. On August 23, 1962, National Security Adviser McGeorge Bundy issued Memorandum No. 181, proposing to engineer an internal revolt.

This was an insurgency operation from the wilder shores of lunacy—Lansdale is commonly believed to have been the inspiration for the fictional character Alden Pyle, the protagonist in Graham Greene's 1955 novel *The Quiet American* who is a missionary for "American" values in South Vietnam.

The Mongoose plan contained month by month objectives intended to build an insurgency in Cuba between March and October 1962. It even assigned a role to Jackie Kennedy, to visit Cuban child refugees in Miami, building on "her impact upon Latin Americans on the recent Presidential visit to Venezuela and Colombia."

Preparation for a U.S. attack was to be paved by a massive program of subversion and sabotage. The CIA's Task Force W, entrusted with overseeing operations, established an espionage and subversion apparatus in Coral Gables, Florida, home of the University of Miami, with a staff of over three hundred and responsible for some 2,000 Cuban agents.

During 1962 the United States carried out several military maneuvers in preparation for an attack on Cuba. One, scheduled for October 15, was canceled when Soviet missiles were discovered in

Cuba the day before by a U-2 spy plane. It was to have taken place near Puerto Rico, with the aim of eliminating a dictator named ORTSAC (Castro spelt backward.)

Although the Cuban people suffered terrible human and economic losses as a result of Operation Mongoose, the Cuban Government proved fully capable of withstanding the U.S. assault. The popular revolt that Kennedy expected never emerged, and his quest for revenge only served to unite the Cuban people even more.

Declassified documents on Operation Mongoose can be viewed on the following website:

http://www.parascope.com/ds/articles/mongooseDoc1.htm

Lansdale's plan identified its overall brief as follows:

"The Goal. In keeping with the spirit of the Presidential memorandum of 30 November 1961, the United States will help the people of Cuba overthrow the Communist regime from within Cuba and institute a new government with which the United States can live in peace.

The Situation. We still know too little about the real situation inside Cuba … Time is running against us. The Cuban people feel helpless and are losing hope fast. They need symbols of inside resistance and of outside interest soon …

Premise of Action. Americans once ran a successful revolution. It was run from within, and succeeded because there was timely and strong political, economic, and military help by nations outside who supported our cause. Using this same concept … we must now help the Cuban people to stamp out tyranny and gain their liberty."

Kennedy's Cold War

In speech after speech, Kennedy had based his claim to the presidency on an aggressive Cold War advocacy of American interests against the menace of communism. In reality, his foreign policy views differed little from Eisenhower's administration, but he radiated an impatient activism, catchingt the the mood of the time.

Once Kennedy had taken office he worked single-mindedly for victory in the Cold War—the struggle for the allegiance of the Third World, the space race, the nuclear arms race and the defeat of communism in South East Asia, Cuba and elsewhere.

When the world was divided up among the victors after World War II, the United States accepted the Soviet occupation of the nations of eastern Europe. The Soviet Union also took the eastern territories of Germany, but no peace treaty was signed to resolve the status of Berlin, which had been the capital of Nazi Germany and in 1945 was divided into four zones which were occupied by the Soviet Union, the United States, Britain and France. The Western Allies were not prepared to cede control of the whole city to the Soviets, but for the Soviets it was an affront to have Allied troops a hundred miles inside the East German border.

Stalin tried to force the Allies out in 1948 by closing all land routes into Berlin, but the United States responded by airlifting supplies into the city. Stalin's successor, Nikita Khrushchev, tried to resolve the issue in 1958 by threatening to sign a unilateral treaty with East Germany, but his bluff came to nothing. Meanwhile, some hundred thousand East Germans, many of them ambitious young professionals and technicians, were leaving through West Berlin each year and East Germany was threatened with collapse. Berlin was becoming a major focus for confrontation.

Although in the late fifties Khrushchev was boasting that the Soviet Union would bury capitalism and that it was turning out nuclear missiles like sausages, the reality was that it was years behind the United States. The Soviets were, however, ahead in the race to conquer space, which was understood by both superpowers to have key military importance. They succeeded in putting Sputnik, the first unmanned satellite, into space in 1957, and on April 12, 1961—three days before the Bay of Pigs invasion of Cuba—Yuri Gagarin became the first man in space. When the American astronaut Alan Shepard went into space the following month, it was only for seventeen minutes, whereas Gagarin had circled the earth for two hours. It would be nine more months before John Glenn would match Gagarin's achievement.

Under Stalin's leadership the Soviet Union never seriously attempted to challenge the United States in its own "backyard" of Latin America. Khrushchev, however, was more adventurous, and as relations worsened between Cuba and the United States he saw an opportunity to wrongfoot the Americans who were humiliating him in Berlin. He secretly approved arms sales to Cuba in September 1959, and when the United States suspended Cuban sugar imports in July 1960, the Soviet Union promptly stepped in with its support by purchasing them instead.

The Eisenhower administration started negotiations with Khrushchev for a ban on nuclear tests in 1958. Even before taking office Kennedy indicated that a test ban treaty was a high priority and that he would like an early summit meeting with Khrushchev. This was arranged to take place in Vienna in early June 1961. En route Kennedy scheduled a visit to Paris, during which he received advice from President Charles de Gaulle to be wary of Khrushchev as he was extremely tough and cunning.

Above: **The Office of the President's Secretary, the White House, May 5, 1961**

Kennedy sought to focus the nation's attention onto competing with the Soviets in the space race. He was still smarting from the failure of the Bay of Pigs invasion, and nervous about his upcoming confrontation with Soviet Premier Nikita Khrushchev. Here he watches on television the space mission of astronaut Alan B. Shepard, with Jackie and Vice President Lyndon Johnson. Three weeks later Kennedy upped the stakes and announced the goal of putting a man on the moon within the decade.

Oh what a beautiful view!

Alan B. Shepard, U.S. astronaut, from space

This is an historic milestone in our own exploration into space. But America still needs to work with the utmost speed and vigor in the further development of our space program.

I am the man who accompanied Jacqueline Kennedy to Paris, and I have enjoyed it.

Left: **The Elysée Palace, Paris, May 31, 1961**

Jack and Jackie arrive for a State dinner hosted by President Charles de Gaulle. Despite strong anti-American feeling, the Kennedys were greeted warmly. But it was Jackie who stole the show, appearing in a gown by American designer Oleg Cassini which looked as though it had come from the latest collection of Pierre Cardin.

Face to face with Khrushchev

After the Bay of Pigs fiasco Kennedy desperately needed a foreign policy success. He bypassed his own advisers and proposed the summit to Khrushchev through a secret back channel: Bobby relayed messages to Georgi Bolshakov, a Washington based Soviet intelligence officer working as a journalist. Kennedy did not wish to discuss Berlin or Cuba, but he offered to accommodate Soviet concern about test site inspections in order to reach agreement on a nuclear test ban treaty, and even proposed a joint space program to keep space out of the arms race. But Khrushchev kept Kennedy guessing right up to the meeting.

Kennedy wasn't at all prepared for the two days of bullying he was to receive. Khrushchev treated him with contempt as a young upstart. He was not interested in discussing a nuclear test ban treaty in isolation from the larger question of dismantling the nuclear arsenals altogether, since to do so would ratify U.S. superiority. All he wanted was for the United States to recognize East Germany. He told Kennedy: "If you want war, that is your problem." He then warned Kennedy that "Castro is not a communist, but you can make him one."

Kennedy was visibly shaken, and he later confided to a reporter that he would have to make a stand, and that the place to do it was in Vietnam.

Right: **Soviet Embassy, Vienna, June 4, 1961**
Kennedy in his meeting with Khrushchev. President De Gaulle, who compared Kennedy to a ladies' hairdresser, warned him to be careful at his talks with Soviet Premier Nikita Khrushchev.

денту Дж. Кеннеди

На память о встрече в Вене

Н. Хрущёв

The Missile Crisis—eyeball to eyeball in Cuba

It seems clear ... that the Kennedy
Administration, under heavy political
pressures, was indeed planning to invade
Cuba in the Fall of 1962, and that the
Kremlin sent the missiles to Cuba to
forestall an attack.

**Kennedy Administration Press Secretary
Pierre Salinger, looking back in 1989**

Right: **Cover of *Saturday Evening Post*, December 8, 1962**
After the world had breathed a long sigh of relief at escaping annihilation, the more bellicose American press celebrated Kennedy's victory as though he had been playing a Cold War game of nuclear chicken.

Next page: **Oval Office, the White House, October 18, 1962**
Kennedy kept a longstanding appointment with a Soviet delegation, even though he had known for two days that Soviet missiles were in Cuba. He listened quietly as Foreign Minister Andrei Gromyko (third from left) complained about calls for an invasion of Cuba that were being made in the United States. Far left: Vladimir Semenov, Deputy Foreign Minister; second from left: Ambassador Anatoly Dobrynin.

The Saturday Evening POST

December 8, 1962   20c

Also In This Issue:
Complete Perry Mason Mystery
By Erle Stanley Gardner
———
Special Recipes For Christmas

"We're eyeball to eyeball and I think the other fellow just blinked."

THE WHITE HOUSE IN THE CUBAN CRISIS

An exclusive account of the historic showdown between Khrushchev and Kennedy

By STEWART ALSOP and CHARLES BARTLETT

After Soviet Prime Minister Nikita Khrushchev had met with Kennedy for the first time in Vienna in June 1961, he came away from the meeting convinced that Kennedy wanted to recover from his Bay of Pigs defeat by attacking Cuba with regular forces.

When Khrushchev proposed to Cuba in May 1962 that it place nuclear missiles on the island in defense against a U.S. invasion, he also had a geo-strategic motivation. The U.S. had placed missiles in Turkey close to the Soviet border, and also in Italy, West Germany, and the United Kingdom. These missiles had become essentially obsolete, since the U.S. was in the process of introducing submarines carrying Polaris nuclear missiles. Nevertheless, the land-based U.S. missiles were a humiliation for the Soviets.

In accepting the offer of missiles, the Cubans insisted that they were doing so for the defense of the socialist camp as a whole. Nevertheless, Cuba had developed elaborate defense plans of its own, and it is certain that it would not have accepted the missiles unless convinced that a direct U.S. invasion was only months away.

If the missiles were accepted in order to deter an attack, it was logical that their presence in Cuba should be made known to the attacker. Moreover, they were not cardboard missiles, some kind of nuclear scarecrow, but were intended to be fired *in extremis.* Under international law Cuba had every right to install the missiles for defensive purposes.

Left: **Television broadcast from the Oval Office, the White House, October 22, 1962**
Kennedy told the American people that Soviet missiles were in place on Cuba and announced a naval blockade of the island, calling it a "quarantine" because under international law a blockade is an act of war.

Castro wanted Khrushchev to announce their installation, but Khrushchev wanted to wait until after the November U.S. Congressional elections. He did not want to weaken the Democrats, in case that would result in Kennedy failing to be reelected in 1964.

The first Soviet troops arrived in Cuba in August 1962, and the missiles began arriving in September. The U.S. could not be sure whether the increased shipments were of conventional armaments or nuclear missiles until one of its U-2 spy planes photographed the installations on October 14. By then some of them, with a range of 2,000 kilometers, were not only in place, but already operational; only a matter of hours would have been necessary to prepare them for launching. Other missiles, with a radius of 4,600 kilometers, were still at sea.

Kennedy was informed that the missiles had been discovered on October 16. By the time he announced this to the world on October 22, Cuba had already mobilized 400,000 armed combatants ready to repulse an invasion, out of a population of six million. The United States had a quarter of a million men ready for invasion, and enough planes to carry out 2,000 missions.

Right: **ExComm members outside the White House, October 29, 1962**
The President set up an Executive Committee of the National Security Council (ExComm) to manage the Cuban Missile Crisis. It included military, foreign policy, and intelligence experts from within and outside the administration. From left to right: National Security Adviser McGeorge Bundy, Kennedy, Paul Nitze, Gen. Maxwell Taylor, Defense Secretary Robert McNamara.

If it had involved only the defense of Cuba, we wouldn't have agreed to having the nuclear weapons installed ... since the installation of those weapons would turn Cuba into a Soviet military base, and that fact would take a high political toll ... I had never viewed missiles as things that might someday be used against the United States in an unjustified attack ...

Fidel Castro, January 10, 1992

... one thing Mr. Khrushchev may have in mind is that he knows that we have a substantial nuclear superiority, but he also knows that we don't really live under fear of his nuclear weapons to the extent that he has to live under fear of ours. Also, we have nuclear weapons nearby, in Turkey ...

Secretary of State Dean Rusk

When Kennedy learned that the missiles were in Cuba, he immediately convened a high level Executive Committee (ExComm) of the National Security Council, which met throughout the next thirteen days, until the immediate danger was past. Its statutory members included Attorney General Robert Kennedy, Vice-President Lyndon B. Johnson, Secretary of State Dean Rusk, Defense Secretary Robert McNamara, Joint Chiefs of Staff Chairman General Maxwell Taylor, National Security Adviser McGeorge Bundy and CIA Director John McCone. Other leading figures, including former Eisenhower Cabinet members, participated from time to time.

Kennedy secretly recorded the meetings of ExComm. The record of the discussions, made public in 1997, provides an extraordinary confirmation of Kennedy's political talents. At the outset the mood, especially from the military and the CIA, was firmly focused on launching a massive military attack on Cuba to take out the missiles before they became operational, and to overthrow the Castro government.

On the first day, Robert Kennedy strongly supported this approach, even wondering out loud whether "there is some other way we can get involved in this, through Guantánamo Bay [the U.S. military base in the east of the island] or something. Or whether there's some ship that … you know, sink the Maine again or something." The Maine was the U.S. ship that exploded in Havana harbor in 1898, providing the pretext for U.S. intervention in the Cuban war of independence against Spain. Such a course of action would, we now know, have led to disaster—the triggering a nuclear holocaust—because some of the missiles were already operational and the Cubans would certainly have retaliated.

On October 22 Kennedy went on television to announce to the nation that the United States was placing a naval blockade around Cuba, although he used the word "quarantine." This was, under international law, an act of war, but Kennedy sought to justify it by claiming that the missiles were offensive, and that they had been placed in Cuba suddenly and deceptively.

Throughout, Kennedy played the stronger hand. He steadfastly refused to recognize Cuba as a protagonist, and brushed aside questions of U.S. aggression against Cuba. Instead, he presented the United States as under attack, and played on the strategic weakness of the Soviet Union.

Kennedy has gone down in history as the man who saved the world from destruction, and it is true that his handling of the crisis took the initiative out of the hands of the hawks in the Pentagon who were pushing for a pre-emptive strike against the missiles in Cuba. But that is only part of the story, because it was Kennedy's sustained aggression against Cuba which led to the missiles being installed there in the first place.

Khrushchev proposed on October 26 that if the United States promised not to invade Cuba, or to support any other forces planning to do so, the Soviet military specialists in Cuba would disappear. The next day he followed up with an offer to withdraw the Soviet missiles from Cuba if the United States withdrew its missiles from Turkey.

Kennedy's reply was that first work should "cease on offensive missile bases in Cuba," and then they could talk about "broader questions of European and world security." Khrushchev chose to read Kennedy's message as promising that no invasion of Cuba would take place, and he agreed to Kennedy's request, even though in fact Kennedy had made no promises at all. Even so, on the U.S.

side some of the military chiefs continued to call for invasion. Cuba was left with no guarantees that the United States would not invade. The United States maintained its naval blockade for another month, and sabotage operations against Cuba continued.

The United States also pressured the Soviet Union for on-site inspections in Cuba to prove that the weapons really were removed. Khrushchev had accepted inspections in his letters to Kennedy, and the Soviets tried hard to convince Cuba to permit them. But Cuba, furious at being left in the lurch by its ally, refused. In subsequent declarations made at the United Nations, the Soviets gave credence to the idea that the United States had promised not to invade Cuba, because this helped it to save face.

During the coming months a process of détente began to emerge between the two superpowers, and the United States even began to sell surplus wheat to the Soviets. But the arms race, far from being over, continued to gather pace.

Next page: **Meeting of ExComm, Cabinet Room, the White House, October 29, 1962**
Members of Excomm meet on the final day of the crisis.

Stevenson: "Do you, Ambassador Zorin, deny that the U.S.S.R. has placed and is placing medium and intermediate range missiles and sites in Cuba?"

Zorin: "I am not in an American court room, sir, and therefore I do not wish to answer a question that is put to me in the fashion in which a prosecutor does."

United Nations, New York, October 25, 1962

Above: **United Nations, New York, October 25, 1962**
At this famous meeting, U.S. ambassador to the U.N., Adlai Stevenson, showed the Russian missile sites in Cuba that had been discovered by reconnaissance flights over the island. This was Stevenson's greatest hour, and the phrase an "Adlai Stevenson moment" has entered the vocabulary of U.S. politics.

Interview with Carlos Lechuga

CUBAN AMBASSADOR TO THE UNITED NATIONS DURING
THE MISSILE CRISIS

Havana, January 2005

You were in New York in the early sixties?
I went there in 1962 when the Missile Crisis
began. I was Cuba's ambassador in Mexico,
then, when the U.N. General Secretary
U Thant visited Cuba, my government called
me and I participated in the discussions with
U Thant and afterward went to New York as
Ambassador to the United Nations for the
negotiations over the Crisis.

U Thant was participating in the discussions, and it was
intended that Cuba would participate, and of course the United
States, but in the event Cuba didn't participate because the
United States did not want us to be part of the discussions. Only
the Soviets and the Americans negotiated. The United Nations
was also sidelined. Not even U Thant took part. He spoke with
me, he spoke with the Soviets, with the Americans, but he didn't
participate in the negotiations. We thought that we would go to
the Security Council with the Americans and the Soviets.

But the Americans and the Soviets made their agreement
without taking any notice of us and then sent a letter to the
Security Council saying the problem was solved. On the agenda
of the Security Council there was an item on The Missile Crisis,
and there were many countries, especially the non-aligned, from
Africa, Asia and some from Latin America with an interest in
discussing the problem at the United Nations, especially so as to

find a formula to resolve the differences between Cuba and the United States.

But they couldn't do anything either, because the Soviets and the Americans simply agreed between themselves, they got rid of the problem and we couldn't go to the Security Council to discuss the resolution of the crisis, and that was how it all ended.

And afterward they agreed among themselves. They signed the U.S.-British-Soviet treaty, the treaty on atmospheric tests and nuclear arms, then came another treaty, then another establishing the hotline between Washington and Moscow.

And then came the Cold War. Cuba did not trust the promise Kennedy made to the Soviets that he would not invade Cuba, because they continued to infiltrate terrorists into Cuba, spies, U.S. naval maneuvers near our shores, the same as before. In fact they did not invade Cuba, as you know … Then came Kennedy's initiative to have discussions with Cuba, to see if it was possible to change U.S. policy and normalize relations.

In fact we were the ones who began the discussions, in conversations between myself and Ambassador William Attwood, who was adviser to the U.S. delegation at the United Nations. Attwood told me that Kennedy wanted to keep these conversations secret even within the U.S. government itself. For example, the State Department did not participate, and not even Secretary of State Dean Rusk, who was a member of Kennedy's inner circle, participated. Lisa Howard, a journalist with ABC. television who had been in Cuba, was the one who acted as intermediary to present me to Attwood.

Kennedy had already given approval for a representative of the Cuban government to go to Key West, or somewhere in Florida, to start discussions, because he did not want Attwood to go to Cuba—it would have been immediately known that an American ambassador was in Cuba and Kennedy didn't want this to get out. Attwood told me that the only people to know about this were U.S. Ambassador to the U.N., Adlai Stevenson, Robert Kennedy, and one of Kennedy's advisers. Before going to Dallas, Kennedy told his office that when he returned he wanted to know what stage discussions had reached with me in New York.

A French journalist from the magazine *Le Nouvel Observateur*, Jean Daniel, was on his way to Cuba and Attwood learned that he wanted to speak with Kennedy while in Washington. Daniel wanted to talk about Vietnam, but Kennedy said they were going to talk about Cuba. "Go to Cuba and speak with Castro, and when you return, come and see me and tell me what Castro has to say." When Daniel was in Cuba speaking with Fidel, in Varadero beach resort, they heard the news that Kennedy had been shot, and so we never found out what Kennedy was going to ask the Cuban government.

It has been suggested—but without any evidence—that Kennedy was going to ask for the withdrawal of the Soviet military group from Cuba. Even as the conversations were taking place in New York, the sabotage against Cuba was continuing. And on the day that Kennedy died, the CIA was handing over to Rolando Cubela in Paris a poison to use in an assassination attack on Fidel. All this was carrying on independently of the discussions we were having. But evidently Kennedy wanted to change the policy, although we don't know what he was going to ask. Depending on what he was going to ask, Cuba would have decided whether to accept or not.

Fabián Escalante has written that the U.S. intelligence services knew as early as mid-September 1962 that there were missiles in Cuba, that is, a month before the Missile Crisis erupted. Did you know anything of that?

I cannot say, but I think it was later than that. But before Kennedy spoke publicly, he already knew the missiles were in Cuba, I don't know how they knew, because only after they knew did they send the U-2 spy planes. It is said that German intelligence informed the Americans that the Soviet ships that were sailing to Cuba had a cargo that, although they didn't know exactly what it was, seemed to them to be missiles. Also some Cubans who had recently emigrated to the United States spoke of having seen suspicious things, large boxes. Then they sent the U-2s in October which photographed the missile sites. That is when Kennedy announced the missiles were in Cuba.

Is it possible that Kennedy was in a trap? He asked Khrushchev personally if he was sending missiles and Khrushchev said no, and Kennedy told Congress that. Then suddenly they found the missiles. That's possible. What happened was also influenced by internal politics. Because there were members of the government who wanted to negotiate with the Soviets—but not with Cuba, they never wanted to talk with Cuba. After the crisis erupted, and before making the naval blockade of the island, they wanted to negotiate, but Kennedy, as he was preparing to be reelected, he didn't want the right wing and the Republicans to have an excuse for attacking him. So instead of solving the crisis through diplomatic channels, in the United Nations, with bilateral discussions, he imposed the naval blockade.

There was a discussion about how to describe the measure, as a blockade or a quarantine, because blockade signified an act of war, and they didn't wish to state that publicly. Instead of calling it a naval blockade they called it a quarantine, which is a commercial term—Kennedy did not wish to give the impression that it was an act of war against the Soviet Union. When the crisis began I thought that there was a risk of war. Then when I reached New York and was involved in discussions, my assessment changed and I had the impression that neither the Soviets nor the Americans were going to go to war.

But surely the military wanted to make war? The U.S. Joints Chiefs of Staff, for example.

Yes, they wanted to make war, but there were other forces in the United States and the Soviet Union that didn't want war—a nuclear war. A conventional war, perhaps, but no one wanted to start a nuclear war, and that was the impression I got in New York when I spoke with the Soviets, and when I spoke with the Secretary General of the United Nations. One time Mikoyan came on his way from Cuba, to meet with the American negotiators, and I breakfasted with him.

He did not say explicitly that there would not be a war, but he gave me the impression that neither they nor the Americans would go to the extreme of war. In the first days I thought there was a real danger, but after some weeks passed, I came to the conclusion that neither wanted war.

What were your impressions of Kennedy at the beginning of his Presidency? And how did he change?

It is difficult to know, but Kennedy was a liberal in the American style. He had problems with the conservative elements at a certain time, because he tried to prevent the attacks on the blacks in the southern states. Also, he gave a speech at the American University, a conciliatory speech, and then he made an aggressive speech in Berlin, against the Soviets, against the communists, against Cuba, against everybody. He changed position. I think he did it according to the pressures he faced in the United States. He was a type who did not have a clear line in that respect. After the Bay of Pigs he had problems with the leaders of the CIA, he also had problems with the Pentagon, that is to say, he was an individual who tried to maintain a policy, but couldn't always stick to it because he was very susceptible to the pressure of whatever influences he faced at a given moment.

Why was that? Because of his personality?

I can't really comment, but it is clear that he was very sensitive to electoral politics. He was planning to be reelected in 1964, and he changed his position according to the political movements and electoral pressures, with an eye to reelection.

Because he did not have a majority in the Senate.

That's right. And he had won the Presidency by very few votes. I believe this influenced him greatly, always thinking of the elections, policy changed according to the pressures he faced. At least, that is the impression I had … As we could never really know, there never was a negotiation, we never really knew what they were going to ask, what Kennedy was going to ask. But clearly he was the one to begin the process of rapprochement. But I believe that Kennedy changed greatly as a result of the political pressures he was under from the right wing, sometimes from the liberals. His mental focus was always on the elections. With Cuba he always had a very tough policy, and it was he who launched the invasion. Especially in 1963, he changed greatly as a result of internal political pressures.

Perhaps there is no way to know definitely because the documents are still classified. But one thing is certain, that in the case of Cuba, those conversations they initiated in 1963 were a risk, and that is why they kept them to a very limited circle.

But presumably even to open the possibility of discussions with Cuba was a mortal sin.

Yes, there is no doubt about that.

Latin America—The Alliance for Progress

During his 1951 tour of Asia Kennedy learned at first hand that nationalist struggles against colonial oppression arose from the basic human desire for freedom, the same desire that had motivated him personally throughout his life and which he held up as the banner against communism. The lesson was spelled out for him in India, where Prime Minister Nehru explained patiently that war would not keep the poor of the developing world from communism. If the United States wanted influence, it would have to address their real needs.

In speeches in the Senate on foreign policy Kennedy went some way towards embracing anticolonial struggles, particularly the Algerian war of independence from France. This, of course, contained an element of *realpolitik*, since the United States had an interest in gaining influence in these countries at the expense of lesser imperial rivals.

A number of programs emerged out of this approach of mixing "hard" power with "soft" power in the first year of the Kennedy presidency. These included: the Food for Peace aid program; the Peace Corps, which sent young, idealistic volunteers as teachers and technicians to the Third World; and the Alliance for Progress, which through promoting moderate reforms sought to forestall revolution in Latin America and promote representative democracy.

The Alliance for Progress was launched at a meeting of the Organization of American States in Punta del Este, Uruguay, in August 1961. The United States had not yet had Cuba expelled from the OAS, and Fidel Castro sent Che Guevara to present Cuba's approach. Guevara warned the other nations of Latin America against being converted into "appendices of imperialism in preparation for a new and terrible war" and attacked the Alliance for Progress as "financial bribery". Cuba, he said, offered a better model for economic development.

While at the meeting Che Guevara spoke privately with Kennedy aide Richard Goodwin. Kennedy cannot have been thrilled when Goodwin relayed Guevara's thanks for the failed Bay of Pigs invasion of Cuba four months before: "it had been a great political victory for them—enabled them to consolidate—and transformed them from an aggrieved little country to an equal."

The economic centerpiece of the Alliance for Progress was land reform. But the problem was that, in the conditions of Latin America, even taking underutilized land and distributing it to landless farmers threatened the interests of the wealthy owners who were the natural political allies of the United States.

The more benign aspects of the Alliance for Progress soon withered on the vine, despite being backed with real U.S. money. The focus switched to the training and equipping of local police and armed forces for counterinsurgency operations. The United States had supplied Latin American governments with military hardware since World War II; what was new under Kennedy was that they were trained and equipped for internal security, to destroy opposition whether it came from landless peasants, trade unionists, social workers, priests, or human rights activists.

The Kennedy Administration developed the practice of overthrowing democratically elected governments it considered "soft on communism." In Brazil the way was prepared for the military to overthrow the reformist Goulart government, which it did in early 1964. This was the beginning of a political campaign by the United States which led to the installation of murderous regimes throughout Latin America in the coming decades.

I have called on all people of the hemisphere to join in a new Alliance for Progress ... a vast cooperative effort, unparalleled in magnitude and nobility of purpose, to satisfy the basic needs of the Latin American people for homes, work and land, health and schools.

Left: **La Morita, Venezuela, December 16, 1961**

At a ceremony to redistribute land under President Betancourt's agrarian reform program, Jackie followed her husband with a speech in Spanish that was televised nationally. In March, Kennedy had launched an initiative named the Alliance for Progress—a Marshall Plan for Latin America—to counter the influence of the 1959 Cuban Revolution, which was immensely popular throughout the region.

... the largest and most impressive land reform program in the entire history of the hemisphere.

Right: **Los Pinos, Mexico, July 1962**

Kennedy is showered with confetti as he travels through Mexico with Mexican President Adolfo López in a motorcade. He praised the liberating impact of the Mexican Revolution. But that had been half a century before, and talk of land reform—the centerpiece of Kennedy's Alliance for Progress—soon became muted as it became clear that it would undermine the ruling elites which were the cornerstone of the United States' anti-Communist strategy in Latin America. Middle class revolution from above quietly disappeared from U.S. policy and was replaced by counter-insurgency to root out political resistance to U.S. plans.

Kennedy at the Berlin Wall

Kennedy's June 1961 Vienna summit with Khrushchev was the second foreign policy disaster of his administration, and he had only been in office four months. His response was to step up his rhetoric against Soviet totalitarianism in public, while compromising privately with the Soviets.

Kennedy had asked his advisers before the summit for a report on his options in Berlin and had been told that there was no solution short of the reunification of Germany, which was not on the cards. He understood even before he went to Vienna that Berlin was not the place to make a stand against Khrushchev. So after Vienna he launched a public relations exercise to regain lost ground.

He announced six new combat ready divisions for European duty, tripled the draft calls, and won approval from Congress for an extra £3.2 billion of military spending and for the right to call up reserves. West Berlin, he told the nation in a televised speech, "is the great testing place of Western courage and will." America must "have a wider choice than humiliation or all-out nuclear action."

In an extraordinary piece of political theater, Kennedy won an appropriation of $200 million for civil defense. Children at school were taught to hide under their desks when they heard nuclear warning sirens, and citizens were enjoined to build nuclear fallout shelters in their basements and backyards. Military leave was canceled and the Strategic Air Command was put on high alert.

Most Americans believed that nuclear war with the Soviet Union was at hand and that the nation should stand firm behind its president. Polls showed that as many as 85% were in favor of keeping troops in West Berlin, while two-thirds favored sending troops to fight their way into the city if necessary.

Khrushchev's solution to the problem was to close off East Germany from the West. On August 13 a barbed wire fence was thrown up along the twenty-seven mile border, later to be replaced by a concrete wall. Kennedy did not make any move to prevent this from happening, and it is likely that Khrushchev understood in advance that he wouldn't. The Berlin Wall was to stand for the next twenty-eight years.

There was only one incident when Soviet and American troops came close to firing on one another. In October 1961 an American commander decided to go to the opera with his wife in East Berlin and as they drove through Checkpoint Charlie—the crossing point between West and East—he refused to show his passport since the United States did not recognize East Germany. As things escalated, Soviet and U.S. tanks, with authorization to fire on each other, faced off across the divide.

The Berlin Wall provided the United States with a graphic propaganda image of the inferiority of the communist system which it exploited to the hilt. When Kennedy visited Berlin in June 1963 he taunted the Soviets by asking what kind of system is it that has to build a wall to stop its people leaving. He declared himself a Berlin citizen himself—"Ich bin ein Berliner."

Two thousand years ago the proudest boast was "civis Romanus sum." Today, in the free world, the proudest boast is "Ich bin ein Berliner." ... There are many people in the world who really don't understand, or say they don't, what is the great issue between the Free World and the Communist world. Let them come to Berlin.

Left: **Wall separating East from West Berlin, West Berlin, June 26, 1963**
Kennedy made perhaps the most successful speech of his political career to a massive open air crowd in West Berlin. Although the United States came to accept the status quo of a divided Germany and a divided Berlin, the Berlin Wall, erected to prevent East German citizens fleeing to the West, became one of the most potent symbols of the Cold War.

Next page: **Checkpoint Charlie, West Berlin, June 26, 1963**
Willy Brandt (left), Mayor of West Berlin and future Chancellor of West Germany, and Brigadier General Frederick O. Hartel (right) accompany Kennedy past the American checkpoint.

Saving Vietnam from itself

The escalation of a U.S. terror campaign against the people of Vietnam occurred on Kennedy's watch, and the resulting mass murder and ecological destruction of the country is the most horrific legacy of his presidency. By the end of the war two million Vietnamese civilians and 1.1 million resistance fighters had been killed, and 300,000 more were missing in action. The army of the U.S. client regime in South Vietnam lost 225,000. Hundreds of thousands more were killed in neighboring Laos and Cambodia. The United States lost 58,000 soldiers, with a further 2,000 missing in action.

Kennedy had became interested in Indochina early in his political career. In a 1956 speech he said: "Vietnam represents the cornerstone of the Free World in Southeast Asia … Burma, Thailand, India, Japan, the Philippines and, obviously, Laos and Cambodia are among those whose security would be threatened if the red tide of communism overflowed into Vietnam."

Right: **News conference, Washington D.C., March 23, 1961**
Laos, a tiny nation of two million people bordering China and Vietnam, had suddenly become the frontline in the struggle against the "red tide."

Next page: **The Oval Office, the White House, June 14, 1961**
Kennedy meets with Nguyen Dinh Thuan, chief minister in the government of South Vietnamese President Ngo Dinh Diem.

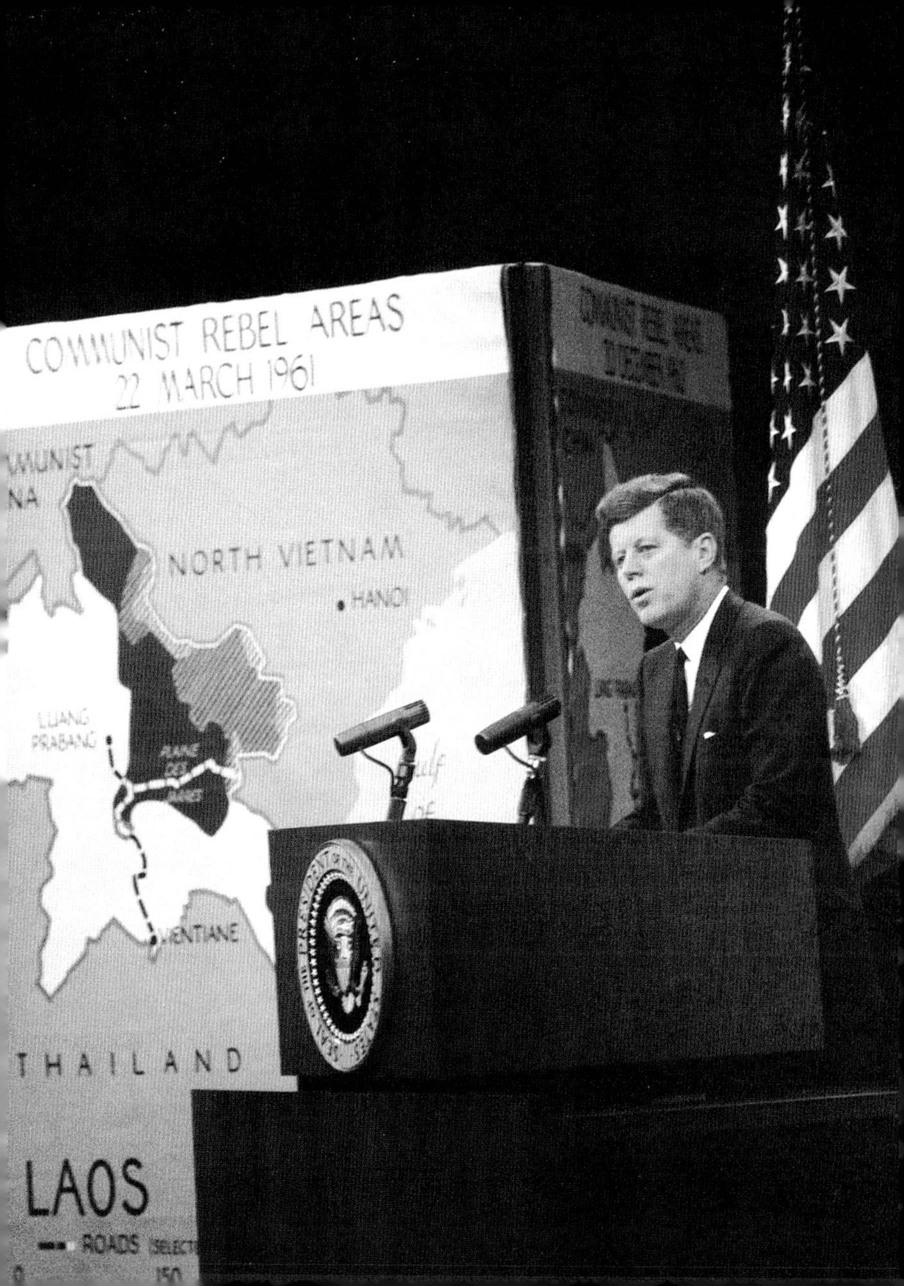
COMMUNIST REBEL AREAS
22 MARCH 1961
NORTH VIETNAM
HANOI
LUANG PRABANG
THAILAND
LAOS
ROADS

After Mao Tse Tung's Communists won control of China in 1949, Kennedy worried that the U.S. had not done enough to prevent their victory. Many of his House and Senate speeches in these years were on the theme of wooing the countries of the Third World with economic aid to prevent them coming under the influence of the Soviet Union and China, and being prepared to intervene with force if that didn't work.

In October 1951, as a young Congressman, Kennedy visited Indochina, where the French were fighting a last ditch battle to hold on to their colony of Vietnam. In Saigon he was briefed by the U.S. Embassy that the French would lose to the nationalist army of Ho Chi Minh, and he concluded even then that the U.S. would have to take over from the French, whom they began to back financially in that year. But when the French were close to their final defeat at Dien Bien Phu in 1954, President Eisenhower resisted pressure from his Joint Chiefs of Staff to intervene. The U.S. war in Korea had only ended the previous year, and it was judged that public opinion was not ready for another war so soon.

At the subsequent peace conference in Geneva, which partitioned Vietnam into North and South and provided for elections for the whole country in 1956, the U.S. refused to sign the Accords. Instead they encouraged the South Vietnamese to block the elections because, as Eisenhower admitted, "Ho Chi Minh would win 80 per cent of the vote."

When Kennedy finally won a place on the Senate Foreign Relations Committee in 1957, an important bridgehead for his assault on the Presidency three years later, he already had an inside track on Vietnam. His father had befriended Ngo Dinh Diem—a fervent Vietnamese anticommunist whom French President Charles de Gaulle considered utterly demented—after he fled Vietnam for a

Catholic seminary in New York. Joe Kennedy helped finance the lobby group American Friends of Vietnam, and JFK was the principal speaker at its symposium in 1956. Diem, a representative of the Catholic elite, was the U.S.'s choice to head its puppet regime in South Vietnam. He immediately launched a campaign of state terror against the majority Buddhist population.

A week after JFK's inauguration as President, the State Department presented him with a report by Brigadier General Edward Lansdale, who had headed a team of U.S. soldiers and intelligence officers in Vietnam since 1954. This stated that Diem's government was losing the fight, a verdict soon confirmed by Defense Secretary Robert McNamara who, along with the Joint Chiefs, National Security Adviser McGeorge Bundy, his deputy Walt Rostow and Secretary of State Dean Rusk, advised Kennedy to send in combat troops.

Concerned that too open an intervention would make the situation worse for Diem, that it would affect the standoff with the Soviet Union in Berlin, and that public opinion at home would be opposed, Kennedy decided instead on a clandestine approach. By the end of the year there were 2,200 U.S. "advisers" assigned to South Vietnamese combat units, two fully operational helicopter companies, and air force "trainers" flying combat missions.

Next page: **The Oval Office, the White House, September 23, 1963**
U.S. Army Chief of Staff General Maxwell Taylor and Secretary of Defense Robert McNamara confer with Kennedy before leaving for Vietnam to review the military situation.

From January 1962 U.S. aircraft sprayed herbicide defoliants in areas where the National Liberation Front was based. In April an elite Special Forces unit was sent to train agents for operations against the North. Kennedy authorized the use of the deadly chemical napalm, which wrought havoc among civilians and resistance fighters throughout the war. None of this was known at the time by the American public.

In March, U.S. officials publicly announced for the first time that U.S. pilots were engaged in combat missions. By October, the *New York Times* reported, "in 30 percent of all the combat missions flown in Vietnamese Air Force planes, Americans are at the controls."

By 1963 U.S. commanders were encouraged that their campaign in the countryside, based on herding seven million peasants into "strategic hamlets"—effectively concentration camps—was working, and foresaw imminent victory and the possibility of bringing U.S. troops home. In the towns, however, Diem's government proved incapable of controlling a wave of protests led by Buddhist monks, several of whom burned themselves alive in front of U.S. journalists. Diem reacted by savagely attacking Buddhist temples.

But Diem's main crime in U.S. eyes was that he and his brother Ngo Dinh Nhu had had informal talks with the North aimed at establishing a neutral regime in the South, with a reduced U.S. role and possibly complete U.S. withdrawal. Nhu told the *Washington Post* in May that "South Vietnam would like to see half of the 12–13,000 American military stationed here leave the country."

At the United Nations, Secretary General U Thant supported a proposal from the National Liberation Front for a coalition government in the South, while General de Gaulle supported the neutralization of the South and eventual reunification of the country.

Kennedy's problem was that political support for his war, already thin, would have been undermined by these maneuvers, leaving him exposed as he began to prepare for the 1964 presidential elections. Diem and Nhu had to go, and so U.S. Ambassador Henry Cabot Lodge was tasked with organizing an army coup. The first attempt in late August failed, but on November 1 the government of the South was overthrown and Diem and Nhu were shot. It is likely that Kennedy warned Diem the coup was coming and urged him to seek refuge in the U.S. Embassy. Nevertheless, he cabled Ambassador Lodge praising him for "an achievement of the greatest importance" that "is recognized here throughout the Government."

"The United States is involved in a war in Vietnam. American troops will stay until victory" … Robert Kennedy said here last week. He called it "war in a very real sense of the word." … The United States seems inextricably committed to a long, inconclusive war … it is too late to disengage; our prestige has been committed. Washington says we will stay until the finish.

Homer Bigart, the *New York Times* February 25, 1962

244

... I don't agree with those who say we should withdraw. That would be a great mistake ... I know people don't like Americans to be engaged in this kind of an effort. Forty-seven Americans have been killed in combat with the enemy, but this is a very important struggle even though it is far away.

Left: **Hyannis Port, Cape Cod, Massachusetts, September 2, 1963**
The subject of American involvement in Vietnam was raised in this interview with television broadcaster Walter Cronkite. Kennedy made his case for staying in the region despite his criticism of Diem's "repressions against the Buddhists."

Arms and dollars—the domestic economy

Kennedy's domestic record is in no way distinct from his foreign adventures. The whole rationale for U.S. aggression against the Soviet Union and ex-colonies of the "Third World"—carefully concealed by the elaborate smokescreen of the Cold War—was to bring as much of the world as possible under American influence as a sphere for trade, investment, and exploitation of natural resources. Similarly, the more advanced areas of Western Europe and a Japanese-dominated Far East were reconstructed after World War II to allow U.S. business to expand.

The military spending that made all this possible prevented the U.S. economy slipping back into depression. Under Kennedy the military budget rose $17 billion above the Eisenhower years, one of the largest and fastest buildups ever. In the summer of 1961 Kennedy called for and got a huge appropriation to prepare for war with the Soviet Union over the "Berlin Crisis". Gore Vidal recalls a conversation in which Kennedy railed against those liberals calling for an increase in the deficit: "Berlin is going to cost us $3.5 billion and that will just do the trick, all the pump-priming they want."

Economics was not Kennedy's first love, but he knew well that presidents were judged on their domestic record and that the electorate expected living standards to rise. During his campaign against Nixon he had attacked the Eisenhower administration for the sluggishness of the economy and the high unemployment rate. Once in power, he knew he must deliver on the domestic front.

Kennedy largely shared the prevailing establishment view—the *credo* of the Republican Party—that the national budget should be kept in balance. But he was more open than most to the ideas of the British economist John Maynard Keynes, who recommended using fiscal incentives and public spending to regulate the economy. He balanced the appointment of Douglas Dillon, a liberal Republican banker, as Treasury Secretary, with the creation of a Council of Economic Affairs under economist Walter Heller, who admired Keynes. Early in his administration there was an economic upturn, so Kennedy was spared the need for radical intervention in the economy. But unemployment remained stubbornly high at over six percent, and in May, 1962, there was a large stock market tumble.

Influenced by Heller, Kennedy became convinced that the tax system was a drag on the economy and urged Congress to cut taxes on corporations and high earning individuals. The theory was that this would stimulate investment and generate higher government revenues as the economy expanded. This would have done little for those on lower incomes or those trapped in poverty, but that was hardly Kennedy's aim. In any case, the Democrats in Congress forced him to abandon the proposal.

Kennedy tried again for tax cuts in 1963, but was again blocked in Congress. Eventually, in September, the House passed a tax-cutting bill, but without closing loopholes that would have generated the extra revenue that would have made it palatable to the Senate.

Kennedy's relations with business were uneasy, and in one instance generated open hostility. The administration was concerned about inflation, and put pressure on the steel companies and unions to forego price and wage increases. But the big steel companies reneged on the deal and raised prices by 3.5 percent. Kennedy was furious, and Bobby flew into action, investigating steel industry expense accounts and possible price-fixing. The steel bosses backed down. But subsequent accounts that Kennedy was "battling Wall Street," bringing the Federal Reserve to heel and championing the underprivileged are purely delusional.

Foot-dragging on civil rights

Throughout his political career, as a Representative and then as a Senator from New England, Kennedy mostly managed to steer clear of the issue of equal civil rights for African Americans, and indeed of most domestic social issues. But as civil rights protests grew in the fifties, it became important for a presidential candidate from the Democratic Party to be seen to take a stand.

Accordingly, Kennedy supported the Civil Rights Bill of 1957 which would, had it passed, have given the Attorney General powers to enforce school desegregation. As the 1960 campaign got under way, he strengthened his staff on civil rights and started making speeches criticising Eisenhower and calling for executive action—action taken directly by the president—to bypass Congress. Discrimination in federal housing programs could, he claimed, be ended "by the stroke of a pen." During his campaign he was able to win public endorsement from well known African Americans such as the actor and singer Harry Belafonte.

One day during the election campaign Kennedy heard that the civil rights leader Martin Luther King Jr. had been arrested and had been sentenced to four months on a road gang for an old traffic violation. He called King's wife, Coretta, and told her: "If there's anything we can do, please let us know." Whether this act was spontaneous or calculated, Kennedy reaped an enormous political reward after his campaign aides distributed three million flyers recounting the incident at black churches across the country.

Right: **LP record cover, 1963**
Produced by *EBONY* magazine, this was a compilation of Kennedy's speeches on civil rights.

John F. Kennedy

AND THE NEGRO

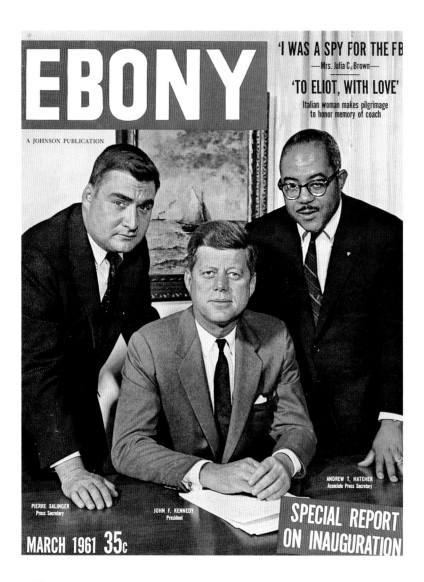

EBONY

A JOHNSON PUBLICATION

'I WAS A SPY FOR THE FB
—Mrs. Julia C. Brown—

'TO ELIOT, WITH LOVE'
Italian woman makes pilgrimage
to honor memory of coach

PIERRE SALINGER
Press Secretary

JOHN F. KENNEDY
President

ANDREW T. HATCHER
Associate Press Secretary

MARCH 1961 35c

SPECIAL REPORT
ON INAUGURATION

In the presidential election Kennedy won more than 70% of the African American vote. This was crucial in Illinois, Michigan, Texas, South Carolina and possibly Louisiana, and hence more important even for his success than the assistance he received from the Mafia in Chicago.

Yet once in office Kennedy showed no eagerness to follow up on his campaign rhetoric, and it was not long before he began receiving thousands of pens in the mail to help him end discrimination "by the stroke of a pen."

It was not that Kennedy had more antipathy to the civil rights issue than other white politicians of the time, or that his attitudes were particularly racist. Like his peers, he had had very little personal contact with African Americans; his closest relations with an African American had been with his valet at Harvard. Civil rights for him was simply part of the electoral calculation, and until its champions forced it up the political agenda it was abstract to him.

The legal basis for an end to racial discrimination had existed since the fourteenth and fifteenth amendments had been added to the Constitution at the end of the Civil War, and the codifying laws enacted in the 1860s and 1870s. But racism against the slaves imported from Africa had been woven into the fabric of society, both south and north, since the founding of the American nation, and would not be dislodged by the occasional court ruling or even by African American participation in the electoral system.

Left: **Cover of EBONY magazine, March 1961**
Press Secretary Pierre Salinger (left) and Associate Press Secretary Andrew Hatcher (right) pose with Kennedy.

After World War II black discontent began to surface in ways it never had before. President Truman, concerned that America's image as the land of the free was suffering, appointed a Commission on Civil Rights in 1946. Then, in 1948, he issued an executive order ending racial discrimination in the armed forces, though this took more than ten years to implement.

The legal breakthrough on civil rights came in 1954 when the Supreme Court struck down the "separate but equal" doctrine which legitimized racial segregation in schools. But once again, real progress was slow, and by 1961 little more than five percent of black schoolchildren in the south went to desegregated schools.

Nonviolent resistance was sparked when, in 1955, Mrs. Rosa Parkes sat in the white section of a bus in Montgomery, Alabama. A bus boycott followed, out of which emerged a new wave of black leaders, including Martin Luther King Jr.

In February, 1960, sitdown protests at lunch counters spread across the South, and over the next twelve months more than fifty thousand people took part in demonstrations in a hundred cities, with 3,600 jailed.

Soon after Kennedy's Inauguration the pace of the movement quickened when groups of blacks and their white supporters boarded Greyhound buses on "Freedom Rides" across the South. Kennedy, preoccupied by his foreign adventures and concerned to retain the support of white leaders in the southern Democratic Party, at first did nothing, standing by while racist thugs beat the Freedom Riders to a pulp. Bobby Kennedy, as Attorney General, refused to back their right to travel, caving in to this flagrant challenge to federal authority from the southern states.

A pattern developed whereby the Administration only sent in federal officials and troops to support civil rights protesters if matters were getting completely out of hand. On January 20, 1961, as Kennedy was being inaugurated, an African American campaigner named James Meredith applied to the University of Mississippi. It was not until twenty-one months later that he was finally admitted, by which time two men had been shot dead and 160 marshals wounded, twenty-eight of them by gunfire. A massacre was only prevented when Bobby Kennedy finally decided to send in 23,000 federal troops.

The Administration was finally shaken out of its complacency when in May 1963 an occupation of restaurants and lunch counters in Birmingham, Alabama, organized by Martin Luther King Jr., was attacked by police. Images of women and children being savaged by police dogs and blasted off their feet by fire hoses went around the world. This was not the way Kennedy, seeking influence in the newly independent colonial nations and excoriating apartheid in South Africa (though opposing commercial sanctions), wanted America portrayed.

The following month Kennedy and his brother took no chances when Governor Wallace announced he would "stand in the schoolhouse door" to prevent African Americans attending the University of Alabama. They federalized the Alabama National Guard and had them escort the students through.

Next page: **Television broadcast, Oval Office, the White House, June 11, 1963**
Kennedy was preparing the ground for a civil rights bill he planned to promote in the fall.

After the shame of Birmingham, Alabama, Bobby Kennedy met privately with the radical writer James Baldwin and a selection of black intellectuals in New York. But from the start of the three-hour meeting the anger was so intense that it was apparent that an unbridgeable gulf had opened between these opinion leaders of the northern black community and the administration.

The Kennedy brothers quickly moved to bring Martin Luther King Jr., the undisputed leader of nonviolent protest, closer to them. But they even suspected King of being under the influence of communists, and Bobby Kennedy had the FBI put wire taps on both King and his attorney, Clarence Jones, who had been present at the Baldwin meeting.

Kennedy played a very astute hand on the civil rights issue, keeping out of the public eye as much as possible, meeting in secret with the civil rights leaders and leaving his brother Bobby to take the heat in his role as Attorney General. He seems to have understood intuitively that the demand for civil rights challenged the power structures of the American state at its foundation, because a legal right, even if granted and enforced, means little if the society is able to adapt and develop other ways to protect the dominant caste. The blacks who had left the south for the northern industrial cities did not face legal discrimination, and yet their access to education, jobs and decent housing and social services was restricted, *de facto,* almost as much as for southern blacks.

The civil rights movement was becoming so powerful by the time Kennedy took office that it threatened to shake American capitalism at its roots. Kennedy's approach was to acknowledge moral entitlement of blacks and embrace their demands just warmly enough for them to be contained. In this Kennedy followed closely the strategy President Roosevelt had developed when challenged by organized labor during the Depression. The New Deal was, in essence, an attempt, successful as it turned out, to defuse increasingly widespread political discontent by getting unemployed people back to work. This is why Kennedy's father—one of the wealthiest men in America and deeply concerned that capitalism might collapse entirely—had backed Roosevelt for the presidency, whereas most of the other leading capitalists opted for the more traditional confrontational approach of the Republicans.

Kennedy recognized that if he were to prevent a collapse of social order he would finally have to provide leadership. A Louis Harris poll in the fall of 1963 found that four and a half million voters had turned against the Administration on the civil rights issue. Nevertheless, Kennedy continued to promote a civil rights bill, which was passed after his assassination. When he learned that Martin Luther King Jr., was planning a massive march on Washington to put pressure on the Congress to pass the bill, he at first tried to persuade him to call it off. When he realized he could not stop the march, he decided to work closely with King to turn it into what the more militant black leader Malcolm X called "a picnic, a circus."

It ought to be possible for American students of any color to attend any public institution without having to be backed up by troops. It ought to be possible for American consumers of any color to receive equal services in places of public accommodation, such as hotels and restaurants and retail stores, without being forced to resort to demonstrations in the street, and it ought to be possible for American citizens of any color to register and to vote in a free election without interference or fear of reprisal ...

Even though we still face the difficulties of today and tomorrow, I still have a dream … I have a dream that on the red hills of Georgia the sons of former slaves and the sons of former slave-owners will be able to sit together at the table of brotherhood … I have a dream that even the state of Mississippi, a state sweltering with the heat of injustice, will be transformed into an oasis of freedom.

Martin Luther King Jr.

Right: **The Rose Garden, the White House, June 22, 1963**
Attorney General Robert Kennedy (center) and Vice President Lyndon B. Johnson (second to his left) with Dr. Martin Luther King Jr. (to Kennedy's right) and other civil rights leaders after meeting with the President.

One cannot help but be impressed with the deep fervor and the quiet dignity that characterize the thousands who have gathered in the nation's capital from across the country to demonstrate their faith and confidence in our democratic form of government.

Left: **The March on Washington, the Lincoln Memorial, August 28, 1963**
Dr. Martin Luther King Jr. addresses a crowd of 250,000 demonstrators from all over the United States. Protest singers, including Bob Dylan, entertained the crowd.

Projecting youthful vigor

Kennedy's health problems were a closely guarded secret from the American public. Whenever adverse stories threatened to find their way into the media—as when, during the campaign for the Democratic nomination for president, Lyndon Johnson tried to fan rumors of Kennedy's life-threatening Addison's Disease—the family publicity machine went into overdrive to kill them off.

Although in constant pain, Kennedy used his quick wit and restless energy to project an image of vitality and vigor, so that only those close to him knew the truth. In his campaign for the presidency he had poured scorn on the administration of President Eisenhower—a man a generation older though much fitter than himself—as being sluggish and hidebound.

But Kennedy's projected image of vigor did not come solely from willpower. It was chemically aided by a fearsome daily cocktail of drugs prescribed by society quack Dr. Max Jacobson which contained hefty doses of methedrine. The Kennedy presidency was, from start to finish, quite literally a presidency on speed.

Right: **Opening game of the 1961 baseball season, Washington D.C., April 10, 1961**
Kennedy throws the first ball of the new season. Vice President Lyndon B. Johnson is on the left, and next to him (in the hat) is Dave Powers, a close Kennedy aide from his early days in Boston politics.

In less than 3 years, we have increased by 50% the number of Polaris submarines … increased by 100% the total number of nuclear weapons … increased by 45% the number of combat ready Army divisions … We in this country, in this generation, are—by destiny rather than choice—the watchmen on the walls of world freedom.

Left: **Hyannis Port, Cape Cod, Massachusetts, August 31, 1963**
Kennedy aboard his yacht the *Honey Fitz*, named for his maternal grandfather from whom he inherited his wit and easy manner. Kennedy's father had established Hyannis Port as the vacation home to which the whole family frequently returned.

It is true that my predecessor did not object, as I do, to pictures of one's golfing skills in action; but neither, on the other hand, did he ever "bean" a Secret Service man.

Left: **Hyannis Port, Massachusetts, July 23, 1963**
There were many photo opportunities when the Kennedys were at play at their holiday home. But with his back in a brace, and his vertebrae disintegrating from all the medication he took, Kennedy must have been in agony playing golf in front of the cameras.

Husband, father, philanderer

An early lover wrote about Kennedy that "he's so singleminded and simple to deal with. He knows what he wants. He's not confused about motives." No assessment could have been truer. Kennedy, his father's "butterfly," had been trained from infancy to focus on achievement in the public world, and at twenty-four his ambition was already being channeled by his father into a political career.

Kennedy was highly sociable, and yet intensely reserved except in the presence of a few close friends. Most of his personal relationships were directed toward aiding his political ambition, in the case of men, or helping him relax, in the case of women. Marriage was viewed as no more than a political necessity. And yet, when he became a father, he opened his heart to his children and was never happier than in their presence.

In early manhood Kennedy developed a remarkable ability to charm and seduce both men and women. From the men he demanded complete loyalty, and he groomed them to be his courtiers. From the women he mostly demanded very little, except companionship and, when not precluded by back pain or his various other ailments, sex.

Kennedy was an avid sex consumer, whose interest was in having a constant supply of opportunities, often procured by staff members such as Dave Powers who had call girls waiting in every city the president visited. Sex was a tic, an itch to be scratched.

Right: **Off Newport, Rhode Island, September 15, 1963**
Watching the Americas Cup race with Jackie aboard the U.S.S. *Joseph P Kennedy, Jr.*, named for Jack's elder brother who died in World War II.

Nevertheless there were some women with whom he seems to have become emotionally close. Many sources have linked Kennedy with a Danish journalist named Inga Arvad whom he met while doing a naval desk job in Washington in 1941. Inga "Binga" as he liked to call her, was four years older than Kennedy, estranged from her Hungarian film director husband, stunningly beautiful, highly intelligent, more experienced than the other young women Kennedy had known hitherto, and with an interesting past.

Inga had succeeded in interviewing Hitler, Goering, and Goebbels, and been photographed with Hitler at the 1936 Berlin Olympic Games. She subsequently had a relationship with Axel Wenner-Gren, the Swedish founder and chief shareholder of Elektrolux and Bofors, the gun manufacturer, one of the richest men in the world and personal banker to fellow Nazi sympathizer the Duke of Windsor. At the personal insistence of President Roosevelt, who from time to time would not so subtly remind Joe Sr. to watch his step, the FBI put Inga under close surveillance as a potential Nazi spy.

The FBI investigators never found a smoking gun, and no doubt, left to his own devices, Kennedy would have kept up his relationship with Inga, who seems to have been the first woman with whom he came close to falling in love.

Left: **Hyannis Port, Cape Cod, Massachusetts, August 4, 1962**
A relaxed and highly photogenic family. John F. Kennedy Jr. ("John-John") was three months short of two years old, and Caroline was nearly five.

Next page: **Hyannis Port, Cape Cod, Massachusetts, summer 1961**
On the beach with Caroline and Jackie.

Children are the world's most valuable resource and its best hope for the future.

Left: **Hyannis Port, Cape Cod, Massachusetts, August 25, 1963**
With Caroline on their yacht the *Honey Fitz*.

He was a warm, witty, bright, nice person who hid some of this under either a lack of ability to expose it, or a desire to hide just how warm and nice and good-feeling he was. Jack would literally beam when Caroline or John-John would come in. He paid a good deal of attention to his children.

Personal friend, Torbert Macdonald

Right: **The White House, October 10, 1963**
With his son, John Jr.

Joe Sr., ever mindful of his sons' political futures, quietly pulled strings behind the scenes and managed to have Kennedy transferred far away, to Charleston, South Carolina.

From then on the FBI kept close tabs on Kennedy, and it is now clear that they had plenty to keep them busy. Rumors have long circulated that Kennedy secretly married a Palm Beach socialite named Durie Malcolm in early 1947. This has in recent years been confirmed by long-time Kennedy friend Charles Spalding, who claims that he was sent to the Palm Beach County courthouse by a furious Joe Sr. to get hold of the marriage papers and destroy them. Not only was Malcolm twice divorced, but she was Episcopalian to boot. When stories about the marriage appeared in Southern racist papers in mid-1962, journalist Ben Bradlee was enlisted to squash the rumors in *Newsweek*.

In February, 1960, when Kennedy was in the Senate and making preparations to run for the presidency, Frank Sinatra introduced him to Judith Campbell, later Exner. She was a close friend of Chicago mob boss Sam Giancana. Campbell had concurrent affairs with Kennedy and Giancana, and later claimed to have acted as a courier between the two men, carrying large sums of cash from Kennedy, and also documents relating to the "elimination" of Fidel Castro at a time when Bobby Kennedy had hired Giancana to do the job. She also claimed to have been a conduit to the White House for payoffs from California businessmen for defense contracts.

In July 1963 J. Edgar Hoover warned Kennedy that the FBI had information that the wife of a German diplomat with whom Kennedy was conducting an affair was a spy for East Germany. The reaction was swift—it was quickly arranged for her and her husband to be sent home.

Kennedy seems to have remained supremely confident that he, and his family, could manage any potential fallout from his escapades, and prevent stories surfacing in the mainstream media. But there was one outraged citizen who came close to scuppering his political career. Florence M. Kater, a woman who rented an apartment to Kennedy aide Pamela Turnure in the Georgetown district of Washington, became incensed at Kennedy's frequent nocturnal visits in 1958.

She secretly taped the two of them, took a photograph of Kennedy leaving the apartment at 3 A.M, and began a letter writing campaign to the press. Kennedy family attempts to buy Kater off through an attorney failed, and she became a one-woman picket at political rallies—including the 1960 Democratic Party National Convention—through into 1961, when she would stand with her placard outside the White House denouncing the adulterer within.

But although the *Washington Star* published a photograph of her, the mainstream press discreetly failed to comment. Kennedy had the last laugh when he appointed Turnure as Jackie's personal secretary. Forty years later President Bill Clinton must have wondered why he could not have been so lucky.

Any number of people could have undermined Kennedy's public image, but during his lifetime it never happened. Instead the American nation, and the rest of the world, watched enthralled as the carefully crafted First Marriage, with two perfect children, glittered with elegance, wit and—Kennedy's favorite word—vigor.

When *TIME* White House correspondent Hugh Sidey asked him for a list of his favorite books, Kennedy immediately mentioned Lord David Cecil's 1939 biography of Queen Victoria's prime minister, *The Young Melbourne*. This was a racy account of the affair between the English poet Lord Byron and Melbourne's wife, Lady Caroline Lamb.

They say on the beach that if the First Lord doesn't **** every day he has a headache. I said "What about the First Lady?" "Oh Jackie doesn't like it that often."

Nancy Mitford

Certainly, [Jackie] had always accepted his promiscuity as perfectly normal, as indeed it was, in the high-powered world.

Gore Vidal

Left: **Outside the offices of the *Washington Star*, Washington D. C., c. 1960**

Florence M. Kater, landlady of Kennedy's assistant and lover—later Jackie's secretary—Pamela Turnure, ran an unsuccessful one-woman campaign from 1959–61 to try to force the Washington press corps to report on Kennedy's womanizing.

But the personality of Lord Byron may have appealed to Kennedy at a more profound level. Both men despised their mothers, from whom they received little affection, and sought comfort in endless love affairs. Both suffered poor health in childhood, and struggled against being outsiders at school. Byron, although he became a lord aged ten, came from lawless stock, and was never accepted by his aristocratic relations, just as the Kennedys, with their underworld connections, were not accepted by the Boston "Brahmins."

After Joe Sr.'s stroke in 1961, Jackie confided to one commentator that if it were not for his father, Jack would never have married her. Jack's apparent indifference to his wife was starkly revealed in the summer of 1956 when he was in Europe with a girlfriend and news came that Jackie had suffered a miscarriage. He made no effort to return home until persuaded five days later that if he didn't, and the press found out, his presidential ambitions would be toast. It was rumored at the time that Joe paid Jackie a million dollars to prevent her divorcing Jack over the episode.

By 1963, Jackie was seldom at the White House, either staying with the children at her horse ranch in Virginia, or away with male friends in Europe. Aristotle Onassis, the Greek shipping magnate she later married, was already part of her circle, and stayed at the White House during the days following Kennedy's assassination. So often was Jackie away that one radio host used to sign off his nightly show by saying: "And good night Jackie, wherever you are."

The Kennedy family "spoke of me as if I weren't a person, just a thing, a sort of asset, like Rhode Island," Jackie confided to Senator George McGovern. Nevertheless, she played the role of political wife to perfection, displaying loyalty and radiant happiness when with her husband on public occasions. The marriage gave her the money and status she had always sought and, as she grew into the role of First Lady, she gained the adulation of millions throughout the world for her beauty, poise, and style.

Although she had no great interest in politics, Jackie campaigned enthusiastically at Jack's side during the presidential campaign, right up to the last month of pregnancy. Once in the White House, she spectacularly set about transforming the image of the presidency with her redecoration of the interior and the installation of a nursery for the children. She organized frequent dinners and concerts, to which she invited writers, artists, businessmen, and intellectuals of all kinds, helping to lay to rest the ghost of cultural inferiority that America still suffered at the time.

On visits abroad, Jackie charmed foreign leaders and the public alike. A fluent French speaker from her student year in Paris, she famously won the hearts of the crusty anti-American French President Charles de Gaulle and his culture minister, André Malraux.

Where Kennedy had a strongly developed feminine side to his character, Jackie, a highly competitive horse rider, was as hard as nails. She was easily a match for the Kennedys. During Jack's life she did as much as anyone to craft the image of the presidency. After he was shot, she stage-managed his funeral and the reception of the foreign guests. And then, while much of the time keeping herself and her children out of the public eye, she assiduously nurtured the myth of the Kennedy presidency that still endures—the Court of Camelot of Arthurian legend, dedicated to chivalry.

Above: **Hyannis Port, Cape Cod, Massachusetts, summer, 1963**
With his father, Joe Sr., after he suffered a stroke that left him
without speech.

I guess Dad has decided that he's going to be the ventriloquist, so I guess that leaves me the role of dummy.

They work in the White House. Their favorite adjective is "Triffic!" They symbolize the regime's youth, bounce, and dash.

In the bouncy capital of the New Frontier, few people pack a springier bounce than two White House working girls known as Fiddle and Faddle ... Though no classic beauties, they have such youthful dash and vigor that everyone in Washington seems to know them.

LOOK magazine

Right: **LOOK** magazine, January 2, 1962

A special issue of *LOOK* featuring life at the Kennedy White House carried a profile of two bouncy "working girls," Priscilla Wear and Jill Cowen, nicknamed Fiddle and Faddle. Washington insiders must have enjoyed the joke. The young women would often be invited by the President at midday to bounce with him in the White House pool.

Marilyn Monroe is a soldier. Her commander-in-chief is the greatest and most powerful man in the world. … It's like the Navy—the President is the captain and Bobby is his executive officer. Bobby would do absolutely anything for his brother and so would I. I will never embarrass him.

Marilyn Monroe to her psychiatrist

Left: **Home of movie executive Arthur Krim, New York, May 19, 1962**
Marilyn Monroe with the Kennedy brothers. She had earlier sung "Happy Birthday, Mr. President" at a democratic fundraiser at Madison Square Gardens, although Kennedy's 45th birthday was not for another ten days. Miriam Makeba also sang at the event. Monroe's $6,000 dress was made of gauze and rhine stones. She had to be sewn naked into it, and it showed. She appears to have been crazy about Kennedy, but such a very public display of affection seems to have led him to end an affair which may have started several years before.

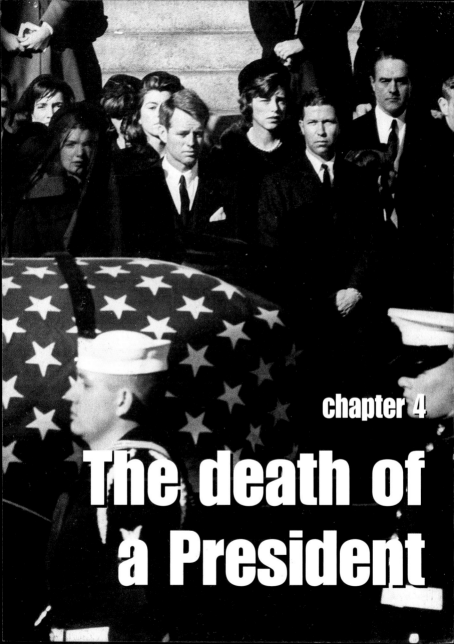

chapter 4

The death of a President

We are entering nut country today.

Kennedy, on entering Texas

Previous page: **St. Matthew's Cathedral, Washington D.C.,
November 25, 1963**
The casket of the President leaving for Arlington Cemetery.

Right: **Texas Hotel, Fort Worth, Texas, 8.45 A.M.,
November 22, 1963**
Kennedy speaks to supporters in the parking lot of the hotel, points up to
their hotel room and explains that Jackie is taking a little longer because
she is "organizing herself."

Next page: **Love Field Airport, Dallas, Texas, November 22, 1963**
Arriving in Dallas before proceeding downtown in a motorcade.

We are waiting for Kennedy the 22nd. We are going to see him in one way or the other. We are going to give him the works when he gets in Dallas.

Bay of Pigs veteran Nestor Castellanos

He knows he is a marked man...

Joseph Milteer, right wing activist

Right: **Love Field Airport, Dallas, Texas, November 22, 1963**
Jackie holds a bouquet of roses that has just been presented to her.

You certainly can't say that the people of Dallas haven't given you a nice welcome.

Nellie Connally, wife of Governor John Connally, to Kennedy during the Dallas motorcade

Left: **Love Field Airport, Dallas, Texas, 11.50 A.M., November 22, 1963**
The start of the eleven-mile motorcade through Dallas.

Mark my word, this man
Kennedy is in trouble, and he
will get what is coming to him.
… Kennedy's not going to make
it to the election. He is going
to be hit.

Mafia boss, Santo Trafficante

The final journey—November 22, 1963

The visit had been planned since June. Kennedy was beginning to look ahead to the 1964 presidential elections, and Texas presented a particular challenge. Despite taking Lyndon Johnson, a Texas Senator, as his Vice-President, he had barely scraped home in the Lone Star state. Worse still, in 1962 Johnson's vacated Senate seat had been won by a Republican, for the first time since the Civil War.

Jackie, who had been absent from domestic engagements outside Washington for most of the presidency, was persuaded to join Kennedy for the trip. Her reception in San Antonio and Houston on November 21 was enthusiastic, and Kennedy's speeches about the space program well received.

There was concern about Dallas, however. A month earlier, U.S. ambassador to the United Nations Adlai Stevenson had been jostled and spat on while visiting the city. Dallas was a stronghold of the extreme right wing John Birch Society, and polls showed that Kennedy was highly unpopular with many ordinary citizens. On November 22, the morning of his visit, the *Dallas Morning News* carried a full-page, black bordered advertisement suggesting the President was soft on communism and a traitor.

The Kennedy entourage arrived at Dallas' Love Field airport from Fort Worth at 11.40 A.M., Central Standard Time. The weather was fine, and they set off in a motorcade of open-topped limousines for downtown Dallas, down Main Street, turning right onto Houston Street and left onto Elm Street. At 12.29 P.M. the motorcade entered Dealey Plaza. One minute later, as they approached an area that has passed into legend as the Grassy Knoll, a shot rang out. At first, those in the motorcade, as much as those lining the street, thought it was a firecracker, or a car exhaust backfiring. But it was followed by more shots, and the driver of Kennedy's limousine, realizing Kennedy had been shot in the head, sped off to Parkland Hospital.

Jackie, seated beside her husband, climbed out onto the back of the limousine and retrieved a piece of his skull. Texas Governor John Connally was in the seat in front of Kennedy and was also seriously wounded, but survived. A bystander suffered minor injuries to his cheek, apparently from fragments of a stray bullet.

In the immediate aftermath of the shooting, most of the police and detectives fanned out to search the area in front of the motorcade, the Grassy Knoll, and the parking lot and railroad yard nearby. Others entered a seven-storey building just behind where Kennedy's limousine had reached at the time of the shooting, the Texas School Book Depository. There they confronted a man in the second floor lunch room less than 90 seconds following the shooting. This man was Lee Harvey Oswald. The police released him when the building superintendent confirmed that he had been working there as an order-filler for two months. Other employees subsequently confirmed that they had seen him in the cafeteria ten to fifteen minutes before.

Kennedy, who had sustained massive injuries to his head, was pronounced dead at 1.00 P.M., and received the last rites. At that time there was no federal crime of assassinating a president, and so the murder should have been investigated as a Texas crime. Just after 2.00 P.M. doctors tried unsuccessfully to prevent Secret Service agents brandishing guns from removing the body before undergoing a forensic examination by the Dallas coroner.

At 2.38 P.M. Lyndon B. Johnson was sworn in as the thirty-sixth president of the United States on board the presidential plane Air Force One at Love Field airport. The plane then flew back to

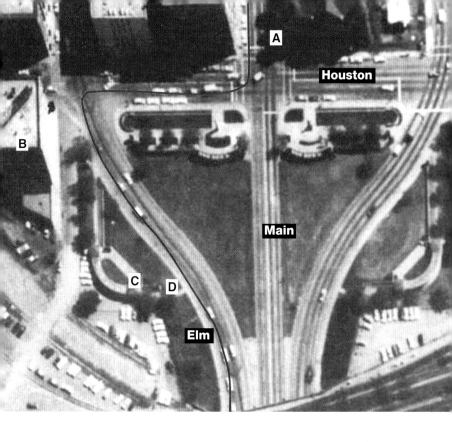

Above: **Route of the Kennedy motorcade, Dallas, November 22, 1963**
The Presidential limousine followed the route marked in red (A), passing
the Texas School Book Depository (B). Kennedy was shot as his car was
approaching the "Grassy Knoll" (D). Abraham Zapruder, an amateur
photographer standing at (C), captured the shooting on 8mm film.

Washington with the new president and the dead president's body on board, accompanied by Jackie in her bloodstained suit, which she refused to change for the rest of the day. They reached Andrews Air Force Base two and a half hours later, and proceeded to Bethesda Naval Hospital where the autopsy was carried out.

At the time of the assassination, six of Kennedy's ten Cabinet members were on a flight across the Pacific for an economic conference in Japan. When they heard the news on the plane's teletype machine they immediately turned back. Kennedy's Press Secretary, Pierre Salinger, recalled that there was almost unanimous agreement on the plane that the assassin would have to be a militant right-winger from the lunatic fringe of Dallas. But then a cable came through pointing to Lee Harvey Oswald as the likely assassin, a man who had defected to the Soviet Union, returned, and established a pro-Castro Fair Play for Cuba Committee branch.

Back in Dallas, police acting on a tip-off arrested Oswald in a movie theater at 1.50 P.M and took him into custody. Six hours later he was charged, not with the murder of the President but with the murder of police officer J. D. Tippit at about 1.15 P.M. Oswald was not charged with the murder of Kennedy until 11.36 P.M. Three spent cartridges and a rifle had been discovered on the sixth floor of the Texas School Book Depository, where Oswald worked.

But Oswald did not live long enough to stand trial. Two days later he was shot in the basement of a police station by Jack Ruby,

Left; **The motorcade, Dallas, Texas, November 22, 1963**
Kennedy and Jackie ride behind Governor John Connally and his wife (top). Secret Service agent Clint Hill jumps onto the back of the presidential limousine seconds after Kennedy is shot and tries to protect Jackie, who has climbed onto the back, as the car speeds away (bottom).

a Dallas night club owner. It later emerged that Ruby had had strong links to Organized Crime since his Chicago youth.

Seven days after the assassination, President Johnson appointed Chief Justice Earl Warren to head a commission to investigate its causes. At first Warren objected, pointing out that it was unconstitutional for one branch of government, the Executive, to employ the head of another, the Supreme Court. But after an impassioned appeal to Warren's patriotism, Johnson prevailed.

Within seventeen days of the assassination, the FBI presented a report to the Warren Commission which argued that three bullets had been fired, all by Oswald. The first, it said, hit Kennedy, the second hit Governor Connally, and the third hit Kennedy.

When the Warren Commission Report was published in September 1964, it concluded that there was no persuasive evidence of either a domestic or a foreign conspiracy. They found that Oswald acted alone, that one shot likely missed, and that one shot—which came to be widely known as the "magic bullet"—hit both Kennedy and Connally.

The only prosecution relating to the assassination was brought against New Orleans businessman Clay Shaw in 1969 by New Orleans District Attorney Jim Garrison. Garrison tried to link Shaw to a conspiracy including Oswald and anti-Castro Cuban exiles. His case collapsed, but it provided many new leads for researchers dissatisfied with the Warren Report.

Right: **Dallas Police Station, early hours of November 23, 1963**
Lee Harvey Oswald, before being charged with Kennedy's murder.

Next page: **Front and back cover of a Warren Commission Report "special," September 1964**

THE **WARREN REPORT** ABOUT PRESIDENT

KENNEDY'S
ASSASSINATION

COLLECTOR'S ITEM 50¢

THE SENSATIONAL
WARREN REPORT
THE WORLD HAS
BEEN WAITING FOR!

NEVER BEFORE
PUBLISHED!
At Last! WHAT
REALLY HAPPENED
IN DALLAS!

STARTLING NEW
REVELATIONS ABOUT THE
MEN BEHIND THE MURDER

96 UNCENSORED PAGES
of BOMBSHELL FACTS,
DOCUMENTS and
PICTURES!

***Was Lee Harvey Oswald alone—or did he have partners?
***Why did he assassinate the President?
***What did Lee H. Oswald reveal in his top secret Soviet diary?
***Who was behind the plot to whitewash the assassin?
***What did Marina Oswald, Lee Harvey's wife, tell the Warren Commission after the assassination?
***Did Lee H. Oswald and Jack Ruby meet in a nightclub two days before the assassination?
***Who is responsible for the wild speculation that has circulated in Europe about mysterious plots connected with the assassination?

THESE QUESTIONS—AND HUNDREDS MORE—ANSWERED IN THIS LONG-AWAITED, UNCENSORED REPORT BY THE OFFICIAL PRESIDENTIAL COMMISSION NAMED TO INVESTIGATE THE ASSASSINATION OF THE LATE PRESIDENT JOHN F. KENNEDY.

Not least of Garrison's achievements was to subpoena the film Benjamin Zapruder had taken of the shooting. This had been purchased for $150,000 by *LIFE* magazine and had never been seen by the public. It was finally shown on national television in April 1975. It shows Kennedy's head forced back by the impact of one bullet, leading many to question whether all the shots came from the Texas School Book Depository behind Kennedy.

In the aftermath of the Watergate burglary of the Democratic National Committee offices in 1972, and the mass protests against the Vietnam War, American public opinion in the seventies became more sceptical of information handed down by government. Dissatisfaction with the Warren Report conclusions led to the setting up of the House Select Committee on Assassinations in 1976, to look again at the assassinations of both Kennedy brothers, Martin Luther King Jr., Malcolm X, and others.

The HSCA's 1979 report, which relied heavily on new acoustical evidence from a recording made inadvertently by a police motor-cyclist in Dealey Plaza at the time, concluded that it was highly likely that there were two gunmen.

Oliver Stone rekindled interest in the assassination with his 1991 movie *JFK*, based around the Jim Garrison prosecution of 1969. The movie pointed to a conspiracy involving Cuban émigrés, the Mafia and the CIA, and presented the assassination as a political coup to prevent Kennedy ending the Cold War and pulling the troops out of Vietnam. As a direct result of *JFK*, in 1992 Congress passed the John F. Kennedy Assassination Records Act. A Review Board was established which, between 1994–98, forced the release of more than two and a half million pages of classified documents, mostly from the CIA and FBI. Many more documents will remain classified until the year 2017.

Opinion polls consistently show that some 80% of Americans believe there was a conspiracy. If in fact there was, and if President Johnson and the FBI did pressure the Warren Commission to defuse fears of a conspiracy, in so doing they may in fact have averted a clamor for war against Cuba and the Soviet Union.

As is clear from a speech by Fidel Castro the day after the assassination, the Cubans feared there would be strong pressure from the extreme right to invade Cuba. The Russians had similar fears. The assassination occurred barely a year after the Cuban Missile Crisis, and at a time when abroad the Vietnam War was escalating and at home the nation was deeply divided over civil rights. There was much to be fearful of.

If I told you what I really know, it would be very dangerous to this country. Our whole political system would be disrupted.

J. Edgar Hoover

Next page: **Commuters read of Kennedy's assassination**

Terrible history has been made here in Dallas, and the magnitude of our city's sorrow can only be measured against the enormity of the deed.

Dallas Times-Herald

There has never been known such intense worldwide grief as is now felt at President Kennedy's death.

The Sunday Times, London

He has been murderously cut off in the prime of life and power; the Nation has suffered another day of infamy which the American people will never forget.

The New York Times

It is a national tragedy of incalculable proportions … What is wrong with the United States that it can provide the environment for such an act? There is a sickness in the nation when political differences cannot be accepted and settled in the usual way.

The St. Louis Post-Despatch

There are those of us who, lacking any real knowledge about how much a man must give of himself when he becomes President, voiced bitterness and hatred toward him … Friday, we were ashamed there had been so many Americans of that kind.

Charlotte Observer

The Weather

Price Per Copy:

NEW YORK
Herald Tribune

European Edition

PARIS, SATURDAY-SUNDAY, NOVEMBER 23-24, 1963

Largest circulation of any American newspaper published abroad

KENNEDY ASSASSINATED

Is Shot Down in Car by a Hidden Sniper As He Rides Through Downtown Dallas; Johnson Quickly Sworn In as President

Shocked World Mourns Leader

PARIS, Nov. 22 - The world tonight mourned the death of President Kennedy.

Radio announcers in West Germany asked as they reported the news. Many ordinary people were left dumb with disbelief. Heads of state sent grief-stricken.

French President Charles de Gaulle, bereaved of the assassination attempts, paid a military tribute at the name of France to President Kennedy.

Johnson Takes Oath In Plane

Woman Judge Swears Him In

By Don Bandolin

MINUTES BEFORE MURDER. President Kennedy, Mrs. Kennedy and Gov. John Connally riding in the fatal Dallas motorcade.

Suspect Kills Policeman, Is Arrested
Ex-Marine Once Sought Soviet Citizenship

DALLAS, Tex. 22 - Police charged

President's Wife Tried to Shield Body

DALLAS, Nov. 22—The scene at the

Gov. Connally Wounded

DALLAS, Texas, Nov. 22. — President John Fitzgerald Kennedy was shot to death today by an assassin armed with a high-powered rifle.

Mr. Kennedy, 46, died about 30 minutes after a sniper cut him down from an upper-story window of a building as his open limousine passed through downtown Dallas.

With wounds in the right temple and the neck, possibly made by the same bullet, he died at story window of a building as his open limousine.

The mantle of the Presidency automatically fell to Vice-President Lyndon B. Johnson, a native Texan who had been riding two cars behind Mr. Kennedy, the 35th President and youngest ever elected to the post.

Mr. Johnson was officially sworn in as President at 2:39 p.m. (20:39 G.M.T.) aboard a plane at a Dallas airport preparing to fly to Washington.

Senator Heard Shots

THE NEW PRESIDENT—Lyndon B. Johnson is sworn in as President in the cabin of the Presidential plane as Mrs. Jacqueline Kennedy stands at his side.

The Washington Daily News

CITY EDITION   **SATURDAY, NOVEMBER 23, 1963**   5¢

It was only yesterday that Mr. Kennedy said:

'This is a very dangerous and uncertain world . . .'

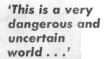

DAILY SKETCH

WAITING GUNMAN HID ON 5th FLOOR, ATE FRIED CHICKEN

KENNEDY ASSASSIN: RED SUSPECT HELD

'Married to a Russian'

By HENRY TROOP

'No! No!' cries Jackie as bullets rip into the car

DRAMA IN PICTURES —Centre Pages

317

In Lincoln's footsteps

It was Jackie who took control of the funeral. Despite the ordeal she had been through, she maintained her poise throughout the coming days. With her heightened sense of occasion, she was clearly determined that the crafting of the John F. Kennedy legacy would begin at once, with the eyes of the world focused on Washington.

Jackie's first decision was that the funeral should echo that of Abraham Lincoln, who had also fallen to an assassin's bullet, ninety-eight years before. The East Room of the White House was prepared to look as it had when Lincoln's body had lain there, with black crepe over the chandeliers and doorways. Lincoln's original catafalque was found, and Kennedy's casket placed upon it. On Saturday, after a private mass for the family, statesmen came to view the catafalque.

The family and media at first assumed that Kennedy would be buried in his home state, at Brookline, Massachusetts, where he had been born. But Jackie thought otherwise. She decided on Arlington Cemetery, the cemetery for veterans from America's armed forces, and visited it with Defense Secretary Robert McNamara to select the site for the grave. Only one other US president was buried here, William Howard Taft.

Previous page: **Newspaper front pages, November 23, 1963**

Right: **East Room, the White House, Washington D.C., November 24, 1963**
Jackie, her two children and Bobby attend the private lying-in-state. A private mass was said, and the casket opened for Jackie to place three notes inside, from her and the children, and a scrimshaw and cuff links. Jackie took a lock of her husband's hair.

Jackie decided that the grave should be marked by an eternal flame. Her inspiration was the one that burns at the Tomb of the Unknown Soldier at the base of the Arc de Triomphe in Paris.

On the evening of Saturday the 23rd, family and friends dined together in the White House. The evening turned into an Irish wake, with raucous jokes and pranks to keep melancholy at bay. But the presence, at her invitation, of Jackie's future husband, the Greek shipping tycoon Aristotle Onassis, was unwelcome to Bobby, who loathed and detested the man.

On Sunday the flag-draped coffin was placed on a caisson drawn by six gray horses and, watched by hundreds of thousands along the route, taken to the Capitol. In the rotunda the casket was lowered onto Lincoln's catafalque. Eulogies were given by Senate Majority Leader Mike Mansfield, Speaker of the House John McCormack and Chief Justice Earl Warren. Jackie and her five-year-old daughter Caroline went forward and knelt beside the bier.

During the afternoon a long line of people filed slowly through the Capitol rotunda. They continued throughout the night until the doors were closed at nine the following morning, some quarter of a million mourners in all.

The casket was brought down the steps of the Capitol on the morning of Monday the 25th, loaded onto the caisson and taken back across the city, past the White House to St. Matthew's Cathedral, past the Washington Monument and the Lincoln Memorial and then to Arlington. Black Jack, a riderless horse with a pair of boots reversed in its stirrups as a symbol of a lost leader, was led behind the casket.

Heads of state and senior political figures had made their way to Washington the day before, from ninety-two countries in all. At noon they joined the procession on foot from the White House, walking twelve abreast behind the Kennedy family. Jackie walked immediately behind the casket, a black mantilla on her head, flanked by Bobby and Teddy. The Kennedy sisters, as was usual, were cast in a supporting role and walked behind. Joe Sr. was too sick to go to Washington, and Rose rode in a limousine.

The moment that perhaps most won the heart of the nation, and indeed the world, occurred after the cathedral service. As the casket was carried down the steps to the street outside, Jackie bent to whisper in the ear of her son, John Jr. He moved apart, straightened, and raised his hand in a salute as the casket passed.

After the casket had been interred, Jackie was handed a burning taper. She leaned forward and lit the flame beside the grave. Then Bobby and Teddy did the same.

A few days after the funeral, Jackie summoned *LIFE* Magazine journalist Theodore White to Hyannis Port, where she had gone to be alone with her children. She told him her husband should be remembered as youthful and vigorous, and that with his death Camelot had come to an end. Camelot? The reference was to a Broadway musical about the Court of King Arthur that had opened the month after Kennedy was elected, and which he had loved. And so the next week White's article duly appeared, quoting the lyrics:

Don't let it be forgot,
That once there was a spot,
For one brief shining moment
That was known as Camelot.

After the poignancy of the nation's mourning, bathos.

Next page: **Washington D.C., November 24, 1963**
Jackie and her two children follow the casket being taken into the Capitol for the public lying-in-state, followed by Bobby.

Mob justice

Oswald's assassin Jack Ruby later told the Warren Commission: "No one … requested me to do anything … The last thing I read was that Mrs. Kennedy may have to come back to Dallas for a trial for Lee Harvey Oswald and I don't know what bug got hold of me … Someone owed this debt to our beloved President to save her the ordeal of coming back."

Ruby was well known locally, to the police and to the criminal underworld. The 1979 report of the House Select Committee on assassinations documented Ruby's connections since his youth with the Chicago Mafia and with the Teamsters Union led by Jimmy Hoffa—a man Robert Kennedy pursued relentlessly. Ruby was later associated with Chicago boss Sam Giancana, the man hired, under Robert Kennedy's supervision, to assassinate Fidel Castro. He also worked for another Mafia leader with casinos in Cuba, Santo Trafficante, and visited him there in 1959. Trafficante was also deeply involved in CIA plots against Castro.

Previous page: **The Rotunda, Capitol, Washington D.C., November 24, 1963**
Aerial view of the casket during the public lying-in-state.

Right: **Police station, Dallas, Texas, midday, November 24, 1963**
No one was—or should have been—present apart from policemen and reporters waiting to cover Lee Harvey Oswald's *(center)* transfer to the county jail. Then Jack Ruby *(right)* stepped forward and fired one shot into Oswald's gut. The scene was watched live by millions on television. Oswald never spoke again, and died soon after in Parkland Hospital.

This charming, complicated, subtle and greatly intelligent man, whom the Western world was proud to call its leader ... snuffed out.

Alistair Cooke, broadcaster

Left: **St. Matthews Cathedral, Washington D.C., November 25, 1963**
The casket of the President is carried down the cathedral steps after the requiem mass, before the journey to Arlington Cemetery.

President Kennedy died as a soldier, under fire, for his duty and in the service of his country.

General Charles de Gaulle, President of France

Right: **Arlington National Cemetery, Virginia, November 25, 1963**
French President General Charles de Gaulle salutes the casket, flanked by Emperor Haile Selassie of Ethiopia *(to his left)*, German Chancellor Ludwig Erhard *(behind Selassie)* and other world leaders.

One of your boys did it.

**Robert Kennedy, to Cuban exile leader
Harry Williams**

Left: **Arlington National Cemetery, Virginia, November 22, 1964**
Bobby Kennedy places a flower on his brother's grave, near the eternal
flame, on the first anniversary of the assassination.

Tributes from international leaders

The death of President Kennedy is a hard blow to all people who cherish the cause of peace and Soviet-American co-operation.
The heinous assassination of the United States president evokes the indignation of the Soviet people against the culprits of this base crime.
... The Soviet Government and the Soviet people share the grief of the American people over this great loss and express the hope that the search for settling disputed questions, a search to which President J.F. Kennedy made a tangible contribution, would be continued in the interests of peace, for the benefit of mankind.

Nikita Krushchev, Premier of the Soviet Union

He was one of the best informed statesmen whom it has ever been my lot to meet but he was altogether without pedantry or any trace of intellectual arrogance.

Harold Macmillan, British Prime Minister

In these tragic hours, all of France is on the side of the United States in its wrath, its sorrow, and also, despite everything, its confidence in the future.

Georges Pompidou, Premier of France

The loss to the United States and to the world is incalculable. Those who come after Mr Kennedy must strive the more to achieve the ideals of world peace and happiness and dignity to which his presidency was dedicated.

Sir Winston Churchill, former British Prime Minister

In the name of the French people, a friend at all times of the American people, I salute this great example and this great memory.

Charles de Gaulle, President of France

Despite the antagonisms existing between the government of the United States and the Cuban revolution, we have received with profound displeasure the news of the tragic death of President Kennedy. All civilized men are always saddened by happenings such as this. Our delegation before the United Nations desires to express that this is the sentiment of the people and the government of Cuba.

**Carlos Lechuga, Cuban Ambassador
to the United Nations**

The death of Kennedy threatens to turn an already bad situation into an even worse one, which can be extremely harmful to the prospects of peace, to the interests of humanity. ...

We immediately foresaw that from the blood of their assassinated president there would be people unscrupulous enough to begin immediately to develop an aggressive policy towards Cuba, that is, assuming that the aggressive policy was not already linked beforehand to the assassination ...

Fidel Castro, Prime Minister of Cuba

Above: from *Bohemia* magazine, Havana, November 29, 1963

The slogan reads: "BE MORE ALERT THAN EVER!"

Interview with Fabián Escalante
FORMER HEAD OF CUBAN INTELLIGENCE
Havana, Cuba, January, 2005

The murder of a president of the U.S.A. is an event of great importance. It is very important to unravel it. Because only by reuniting the past is it possible to live in the present and is it possible to think of the future.

General Escalante began by explaining how he first became involved in investigating links between Cuban counter-revolutionaries plotting the assassination of Fidel Castro, and the assassination of President Kennedy. Cuban intelligence had received information early in 1965 about the activities of Rolando Cubela, a Cuban émigré. After working on the case for a year, Escalante's team established that Cubela had been engaged by a CIA agent, another Cuban émigré named Manuel Artime, to assassinate Fidel Castro on March 13, 1966 while Castro attended an event on the steps of the University of Havana.

We rounded up the people who were plotting to assassinate Fidel on February 25 and 26, 1966. Then, as we gained more information, we discovered that plots had been tried out on previous occasions. In 1963, Cubela had been in France and had tried to meet with a member of the Kennedy Administration. Then in 1975 the Church Report into CIA plots to assassinate foreign leaders was published. It included a report about an agent who, we immediately realized, must be Rolando Cubela. It revealed that Cubela was in Paris in early November 1963 and had met with a CIA official there.

I became head of Cuban security in 1976. In 1978 I planned to present our findings on Cubela at an anti-imperialist tribunal that was being organized as part of the World Youth Festival in Havana that year. During one of the preparatory meetings I had with Cubela, he noticed a report in the national paper *Granma* which detailed the espionage activities carried out from the U.S. Embassy until it was closed in January 1961. He spotted a photograph of one of their diplomats, David Sánchez Morales, in the article and said to me: "This is the man I met with in Paris."

At that time we knew that David Sánchez worked with a CIA agent called David Attlee Phillips who ran a public relations company in Havana as cover. Phillips went on to be the head of the Western Hemisphere Department of the CIA. As a result of my conversations with Cubela, I began to fill in the blanks.

At the end of 1978, a delegation from the U.S. House of Representatives which was investigating the assassinations of Kennedy and Martin Luther King visited Cuba, asking for information on various émigré Cubans living in the U.S. They wanted to interview Cubela, and they also interviewed Fidel Castro.

We began to put two and two together. We knew that Cubela had turned against the Cuban Revolution as early as March 1959. He had been a student leader in the university. He was politically ambitious, and had played an important role in opposing the Batista dictatorship. He was second in command of the Revolutionary Directorate, and had participated in the execution of Batista's military intelligence chief, Colonel José Blanco Rico.

Cubela told me he had finally gone over to the CIA in 1963, while he was in France. The CIA gave him a hypodermic syringe in the shape of a fountain pen to poison Fidel Castro with botulin. The date was set for December 7, when Fidel Castro would be attending a commemoration for the Cuban hero Antonio Maceo.

They were handing over the pen on November 22, the exact day Kennedy was assassinated. In fact, Cubela told me, they were in a safe apartment when the CIA official received a telephone call. He turned to Cubela and said: "Something very important has happened, they have assassinated Kennedy and I need to leave you for a briefing." This CIA agent was David Sánchez Morales, who became head of operations at the huge CIA headquarters in Miami.

Now to turn to the murder of President Kennedy …

In my view, Kennedy was condemned by the Cuban-American Mafia after the Bay of Pigs invasion. They made him the scapegoat for that failure, because he refused to authorize the second bombing of the Cuban airports, or the deployment of the American troops that were in the aircraft carriers and landing craft off the Cuban coasts.

Later, at the time of the Missile Crisis of October 1962, the U.S. Chiefs of Staff wanted Kennedy to make a massive, surprise attack on Cuba. That is when he asked them: "OK. So how many missiles are in Cuba? Are they spread between all the missile bases?" They replied, "No." "And one of these missiles could be fired?" "Well, yes." "In that case, we are going to negotiate."

It seems to me Kennedy made a rational decision, to try to

convince the Soviets, which he managed with success. In my opinion, Nikita's legs gave way beneath him in the end. But the Cuban Mafia were already sharpening their teeth. Ever since the sixties they have campaigned for the implementation of Track Two, that is, for direct military aggression against us. They have never countenanced any other approach to relations between the two countries.

So when the Missile Crisis was not resolved to their satisfaction, they again started accusing Kennedy of betrayal. But in 1963 Kennedy, who seems to have been a pragmatic man, came to realize that direct aggression on its own would never resolve the Cuban problem, that Cuba would not cave in.

And so the National Security Council, under the direction of Robert Kennedy, reviewed various alternatives for dealing with Cuba. These included economic pressure, sabotage, and terrorist attacks, but also to offer the Cuban government the prospect of negotiation with the United States—according to a U.S. agenda, of course. This approach was based on the contradictions that had emerged between Cuba and the Soviet Union during the Missile Crisis: we did not agree with the way the Soviets had resolved the crisis, and the Americans were well aware of that and wanted to exploit those contradictions.

When the Cuban-American Mafia learned of this, they were incensed. The key moment was on March or April 18, 1963, when José Miró Cardona, the leader of the Cuban émigrés, resigned from his position of president of the Cuban Revolutionary Council—an organization that the CIA had created after the Bay of Pigs—

claiming that Kennedy had betrayed them. Then in May Orlando Bosch Ávila, one of the most important Cuban-American terrorists of the past forty-five years, published a pamphlet called *The Cuban Tragedy*, in which he directly accused Kennedy of betraying the Cuban cause.

Of course, Kennedy had other enemies—the big steel companies, those opposed to racial desegregation—but the ones who had the means, the opportunity and the training to kill him were the Cuban émigrés. They had been well trained by the United States in assassination, terrorism, and other crimes.

I believe we have demonstrated—on the basis of information provided by the United States, because we did not know him—that Lee Harvey Oswald was a veteran agent either of military intelligence, naval intelligence, the CIA, or the FBI. Oswald's defection to the Soviet Union in 1959 has no logic except in relation to the downing of the U-2 spy plane on May 1, 1960. Remember, in that month there was to have been a meeting between Khrushchev and Eisenhower, but it was canceled when the U-2 piloted by Gary Powers was shot down.

Where did Oswald work? In the aero-naval base of Atsugi in Japan from where the U-2s were launched. Oswald arrived in the Soviet Union saying he wanted to stay. So were the Soviets, who were suspicious even of their own shadows, going to let Oswald stay in return for nothing? Impossible!

You figure it out: Oswald is an agent of the CIA, or other

intelligence service; he goes to the Soviet Union; he marries Marina Prusakova, then returns to the United States in the middle of 1962 with all expenses paid. He meets the president of an anti-communist organization, goes to Dallas and starts work in a helicopter company, and then in another company producing strategic maps. The FBI opens a file on him, then closes it. How is all this possible? He gets involved with a Russian immigrant circle (as a fluent Russian speaker) then arrives in New Orleans on April 27, 1963.

There he gets involved with two opposing groups, first the Anti-Communist League, directed by a former FBI agent, and then with the Cuban Revolutionary Council which had its office at 544 Camp Street and whose leader was Sergio Arcacha. (Arcacha was a Cuban who had been the Consul in Bombay and was discovered embezzling funds.) One day Oswald turns up at the farm of another Cuban, Carlos Bringuier, and announces that he is a marine and offers to train Cuban exiles to fight against Fidel Castro.

Next he makes himself president of the Fair Play for Cuba Committee, of which he is the only member and which is based in an office that doesn't exist. On August 9 he hands out leaflets on the street, gets into a fight with Bringuier, goes on a radio program and announces: "I am a Marxist-Leninist."

Then he goes back to Dallas, where he meets Silvia Odio, daughter of Amador Odio, a leading counter-revolutionary figure in Cuba who is in jail there at that time. He tells her he is an expert marksman and that "the Cuba problem will only be resolved by killing Kennedy."

Oswald's next stop is Mexico, where he turns up at the Cuban Embassy demanding a visa and creates a scandal. He is told that, as his final destination is Moscow, he must first get a Soviet visa. So he goes to the Soviet Embassy where he is told he will have to wait a year. He goes back to the Cuban Embassy, has words with the Consul, then returns to Dallas early in October.

Later, in Cuba we discovered a mysterious letter that had arrived through our mail system. It was addressed to Oswald and corresponded with other letters that had arrived in the United States from Cuba. In these letters it said that Oswald could put out a candle at fifty meters with one shot.

So what is this all about, if not to link the Cuban intelligence services with Oswald? Kennedy dies and immediately a campaign is launched by the most reactionary Cuban exile organizations … Alpha 66, MIRC, Orlando Bosch—they all begin to accuse Cuba, saying that Fidel Castro killed Kennedy.

Then there was also the incident with Daniel Harker of the Associated Press, who was in Havana in September 1963 at a reception at the Brazilian Embassy, He met Fidel Castro there and asked him what he thought about the attempts by the CIA to assassinate him. Fidel replied to the effect that political assassination is very dangerous because it is a boomerang.

It was several years later, in 1978, that we had the opportunity to learn more about President Kennedy's assassination from a Cuban named Antonio Cuesta. Cuesta was leader of the anti-Castro terrorist group "Comandos L," and had sailed to Havana in a boat with several others, including Herminio Díaz, with the aim of killing Fidel Castro. There was a gun battle with the militia from the Hotel Comodoro, in the Monte Barreto district of Havana. Díaz and one other man were killed. Tony Cuesta tried to get away in a boat which had come from Florida, but the militia fired on it and it exploded.

Cuesta lost his arms and his sight in the explosion, but he was rescued from the sea. He was treated in hospital, then he was tried in court, and sentenced to prison. No doubt he thought we were going to kill him.

Then in 1978, as a result of the first conversations between the Cuban community in the United States and the Cuban government, there was an agreement to release some of the prisoners being held in Cuba. Tony Cuesta was one of them.

As head of Cuban security, I interviewed Cuesta. He was an elderly man, with little education, who spoke very softly and was difficult to hear. He told me that Herminio Díaz had taken part in the assassination of Kennedy, and also another Cuban, Eladio del Valle Gutiérrez, known as "Yito." Yito had been a policeman and later a member of the Cuban parliament under Batista. He was a smuggler who had worked with US Mafia boss Santo Trafficante, and was mayor of a town to the south of Havana named Batabanó where contraband goods from the United States entered the country.

What Cuesta said is more or less as follows—but this happened many years ago;—it's a pity that the conversation was not recorded, but we didn't have the necessary experience or the resources at the time. He already knew he was being freed; he probably felt grateful for the treatment he had received from us and wanted to do something in return.

We started talking with Cuesta about Herminio Díaz, who had come in the launch with him. Cuesta was a seasoned gangster and had assassinated another gangster in the Cuban consulate in Mexico in the fifties. It was then he said that Herminio and Yito were linked with the assassination, and that they were there in Dallas at the time. (They were both wanted for questioning by New Orleans District Attorney, Jim Garrison, who had reopened the case.)

"What do you mean, 'They were there?'", I asked. "Did they shoot him or not?" Because I knew that Herminio had been a marksman. These gangsters were professionally trained marksmen. But he would tell me absolutely nothing. He said, "I can't tell you anything more, because if I do I will be dead the moment I arrive in Miami."

I ask myself why did Johnson clip the wings of the Warren Commission? Why did the campaign to blame Cuba collapse? This campaign was started by Cubans, and other elements, such as journalists linked to the CIA. This was in November. But by the middle of December, a few days later, this campaign has been squashed. We are not the people to explain this, we don't know why. What we *do* know is that something happened, and the U.S. authorities decided that there must be only one person responsible,

My sole aim is to present the elements that we have found for investigation. I am not presenting a theory. My personal view is that Lee Harvey Oswald was not a lone assassin. I believe that the involvement of Oswald was linked to a plot to incriminate Cuba and Fidel Castro in the Kennedy assassination. What I *do* claim is that Oswald was an agent of the U.S. intelligence services. And what I also claim is that all those whom Oswald was associated with from the time he arrived in New Orleans until he was arrested in Dallas were Cuban counter-revolutionaries.

There is not the slightest doubt that Oswald was assassinated, and that he was assassinated in a police station, and by a representative of Organized Crime. Because Jacob Rubenstein, alias Jack Ruby, was a member of the Chicago Mafia family of Sam Giancana and John Rosselli.

So for what reason was Jack Ruby in Havana in 1959? Because it was his job to get out all the money from the casinos.

He was here in August or September 1959, and the following year we received information about his visit. Santo Trafficante was in jail here, until January 1960 when he was expelled from the country.

Already, in 1959, a counter-revolutionary organization had been formed. This was the Anti-Communist Militia under the leadership of Rolando Masferrer, and of which Eladio ("Yito") del Valle was a member. We had infiltrated our own agent into it, a man named Juan Sacornal, and he kept us informed of their plots. At that time Masferrer and Yito were confined to Miami. The U.S. authorities did not let them leave the city because they had committed various terrorist acts. Another of our agents, Luis Tacornal, who went under the name Fausto, was the link between Masferrer, Yito, and their people in Havana and New Orleans. He was a Cuban émigré who had studied in New Orleans and lived there.

It was Fausto who reported to us that Jack Ruby was connected with Masferrer, but in 1960 the name Ruby meant nothing to us. It was only in the nineties, when we were revising the file on Tacornal, which was code named Opera, that we came upon a report from Tacornal which spoke of contacts between Ruby and Yito. By this time both Tacornal and Ruby were dead.

It is quite impossible that the assassination of a president could be carried out by one man. It was not a simple operation, but something very complex. Always in a clandestine operation of this kind many situations are going to arise that could not have been foreseen, and for one simple reason: you prepare a plot, but within it there are hundreds of people who know nothing about it.

The Warren investigation collected a large quantity of information, much of which they didn t analyze, because they didn t want to.

There are several examples: For instance, those tramps who were detained by the police and then mysteriously disappeared. Or the case of the policeman Tippit, a man who had joined the police force only two months before. What does Tippit have to do with it? They said that Oswald killed him, but he couldn't have done because the two men were in completely different places. Oswald went to his house to change his clothes, and then, after supposedly committing the assassination, he goes to a cinema, armed with a revolver. It all makes no sense, no sense at all.

The Cuban-American Mafia had wanted more. Remember that this Mafia want to grind us into the dust. Since they left in 1959, they have wanted to destroy Cuba. They are not interested in discussions with anyone in Cuba. They know there is only one way that they can return and recover what they lost, for a logical reason: forty-six years later, who is going to come and throw you out of your house, after a whole generation has died? This is a very powerful Mafia, with its members in the Senate, in the House of Representatives, and so on.

If you analyze U.S. policy in the last twenty years since President Ronald Reagan was in power, you will realize that it does have a precedent—and that it is a throwback to McCarthyism. So, U.S. policy has experienced an extraordinary involution. And that is why it is so important that we should determine the causes of the Kennedy assassination.

I have no doubt that the trail of the counter-revolutionaries leads to solving the assassination of Kennedy. I cannot say that the ones who fired the shots were Cuban, and I have never said it. I have only said what I have been told—that is, the reports, the small pieces of information we have collected.

But the footprints of the Cuban counter-revolutionaries are there. They are there beside Oswald, they are there in Dallas, they are there in Mexico.

chapter 5

icon and legend

The JFK legend

In the brief few years the American public knew Kennedy he achieved the kind of popularity usually reserved for movie stars. Rather than fading when Kennedy became president, this popularity increased, and stayed high throughout the next three years.

Three months into the presidency Kennedy's approval rating had soared to 91 percent. Even after the Bay of Pigs invasion it only dropped to 83 percent, while 65 percent agreed that U.S. troops should not have been sent to Cuba. Kennedy commented: "It's just like Eisenhower. The worse I do, the more popular I get."

More than any previous president, Kennedy made himself accessible to the public, or so at least they felt. Against much advice he instituted weekly televised news conferences, confident that he could handle the press. Whereas as a young man he had often appeared awkward in public, he was now in his element with quick repartee and humorous exchanges.

Behind the well crafted media image there was another Kennedy, a man whose emotions were tightly controlled and who kept a distance even from his closest advisers and personal friends. His aide Richard Goodwin recalled becoming suddenly aware of this other side early in the presidency: "I knew, even then, there was an inner hardness, often volatile anger, beneath the outwardly amiable, thoughtful, carefully controlled demeanor of John Kennedy."

After Kennedy's death he became for many the young martyr, struck down before he could complete his work. The escalation of the Vietnam War under Johnson and Nixon traumatized the nation, and the Watergate scandal under Nixon sapped the last of the youthful idealism that many had felt in the Kennedy years. Jackie's Camelot image and her romanticized vision of the Kennedy court as "a magic moment in American history" caught hold.

With the years some Camelot courtiers have sought to clear Kennedy of blame for Vietnam. Kenneth O'Donnell floated the view that he was secretly planning to withdraw troops and accept defeat. Official Camelot historian Arthur Schlesinger, Jr. entered the lists with his 1978 biography of Robert Kennedy, and later encouraged the views put forward in Oliver Stone's 1991 movie *JFK*.

The heaviest hitter to join the debate was Kennedy's Defense Secretary, Robert McNamara. In his 1995 book *In Retrospect* he said he thought it "highly probable that, had Kennedy lived, he would have pulled us out of Vietnam."

If so, this can only be conjecture. As Dean Rusk, Kennedy's Secretary of State, has written, "I had hundreds of talks with John F. Kennedy about Vietnam and never once did he say anything of this sort." Walt Rostow, Kennedy's deputy National Security Adviser, who never repented the U.S. invasion of Vietnam, asked rhetorically in 1995: "Is it credible that the United States would have withdrawn in the aftermath of a coup and assassination [of South Vietnamese Premier Diem] which were seen by the world to have been carried out with its acquiescence?"

Nevertheless, such is the power of the Kennedy myth that he is mostly remembered as a man of peace who fought for liberal causes.

Previous page: **Artwork from a Kennedy board game, 1962**
Published within Kennedy's lifetime.

Next page: **Kennedy board game, "Kennedy Cards," "JFK Coloring Book," 1962, 1963**
Published within Kennedy's lifetime.

THE EXCITING NEW GAME OF
THE KENNEDYS

COLORING BOOK

What is the Supreme Court?
Daddy says it will look like this one day.
Wouldn't that be fun?
You would never get mixed up.
There are ten men here.
Count them----Ten.
Daddy wants more people working.
Daddy loves everybody.

INCLUDES:
REPLICA OF JFK'S
RESCUE MESSAGE!

PT 109

JOHN F. KENNEDY: PT 109 BOAT COMMANDER

⚠ **WARNING**

CHOKING HAZARD–Small parts.
Not for children under 3 years. AGES 5 AND UP

360

The most burning thing I can remember about Jack is that he was a fighter.

Choate football coach

Previous page: **From JFK Coloring Book, 1962**
A satirical spread.

Left: **GI Joe action figure: "John F. Kennedy PT 109 Boat Commander," 2000**
The manufacturer, Hasbro, donated a portion of the proceeds to the John F. Kennedy Library and Museum.

Web nasty—a step too far

A Scottish company came in for harsh criticism when it launched a computer video game—*JFK Reloaded*—on the 41st anniversary of the assassination. The game provides a detailed simulation of the presidential motorcade as it drove through Dealey Plaza in downtown Dallas n November 22, 1963. It places the player at the sixth-floor window of the Texas School Book Depository, from where the Warren Commission concluded that Lee Harvey Oswald fired three shots and killed Kennedy. The player is challenged to recreate the three shots and can afterward analyse in detail the trajectory and effect of each.

The designers claim that the purpose of the game is to demonstrate that the Warren Commission's conclusion—that Oswald acted alone and fired only three shots—is perfectly feasible. Yet to judge from reviews the game received, hitting the target in the way it actually happened seems to be quite a feat. As for the concept, reviewers found the game, in all its graphic verisimilitude, tasteless and tacky.

Right: **Traffic Management video game *JFK Reloaded*, November 2004**
The publisher offered a prize of up to $100,000 in an online competition for the player who most closely matched the shots that, according to the Warren Commission Report on Kennedy's assassination, were fired by Lee Harvey Oswald.

Of course, there are as many rich Elvis collectors as rich JFK collectors.

Charles E Schwarz

Left: **A German collector of Kennedy memorabilia**

Evelyn's secret shrine

Mrs. Evelyn Lincoln, Kennedy's White House secretary, joined his staff in 1953, and remained at his side until the day he was assassinated in Dallas ten years later.

Parkland Hospital staff in Dallas handed Mrs. Lincoln the late President's personal effects, including his Cartier watch. Back in Washington, President Johnson ordered her to clear Kennedy's possessions out of the Oval Office, and she moved with them into the Executive Office Building next to the White House. She continued to maintain custody of the material until it was moved to the National Archives and Records Office in late 1965.

When the presidential library opened in Boston in 1979 it contained an "Evelyn Lincoln Collection" of papers she had prepared. But neither the library nor the Kennedy family knew that Mrs. Lincoln had created a secret shrine to her fallen President that incorporated hundreds of items, including the flags that once hung in the Oval Office and many of Kennedy's personal possessions. She even came by some of Jackie's dresses, earrings and coats.

When Mrs. Lincoln died in 1995 she left her collection to her husband, and he in turn left them to a family friend and collector, Robert L. White. In 1998 White offered up hundreds of the items for auction, and this provoked a denunciation of Mrs. Lincoln from Kennedy's children, who charged that she "took advantage of her position as our father's secretary, and later as custodian of objects intended for the library."

Right: **Arlington National Cemetery, Virginia, November 22, 1994**
The last of Evelyn Lincoln's annual visits to commemorate Kennedy's death. She died six months later, aged 85.

JFK in the movies

Kennedy has been the subject of an ever-lengthening stream of documentaries and docudramas. But the two movies that have made most impact both came out of Hollywood in the 1990s. Each, in different ways, speaks to a political agenda.

Thirteen Days was released in 2000. It is based on the tapes of the White House discussions during the missile crisis of October 1962. However, by focusing only on the thirteen days of the crisis, and excluding the Russians and the Cubans from consideration, it reinforces the view that it was Kennedy's toughness—facing up to crazy foreigners out to destroy America—that saved the day.

In fact, as Kennedy's Defense Secretary Robert McNamara said in 1989, "If I had been a Cuban leader, I think I might have expected a U.S. invasion. Why? Because the U.S. had carried out what I have referred to publicly as a debacle—the Bay of Pigs invasion. … Secondly, there were covert operations. The Cubans knew that."

As for the Russians, they had witnessed Kennedy oversee the largest military buildup ever in peacetime. The Americans had more than 500 bombers and missiles that could hit the Soviet Union, whereas the Russians had less than 50 that could hit the U.S. What is more, one of the five approved U.S. strategic plans at the time called for a nuclear first strike against the Soviet Union. This was not, perhaps, the preferred option, but the Soviet generals knew about the plan and could hardly ignore it. Placing missiles in Cuba was a far less costly option than trying to catch up in the arms race.

The film's theme follows Secretary of State Dean Rusk's homely observation: "We were eyeball to eyeball and I think the other fella just blinked." But what Khrushchev knew, and Kennedy did not, was that the missiles in Cuba, with warheads nearly as large as those unleashed on Hiroshima, were ready for use. If he hadn't "blinked" the world could have perished. In taking the missiles out he risked political humiliation and hastened his own political demise.

Oliver Stone's 1991 movie *JFK* dramatizes the unsuccessful investigation by New Orleans District Attorney Jim Garrison in the late 1960s into the activities of Clay Shaw, a businessman charged with conspiring to kill the president. It posits a conspiracy involving Cuban émigrés, CIA agents, the Mafia, and top government officials, perhaps even Kennedy's successor, Lyndon Johnson.

JFK revived interest in the assassination, created an uproar in the U.S., and was strongly attacked in the media. But a movie is not a court of law, and *JFK* could not be expected to present a forensic weighing of evidence about the assassination. Writers have always dealt with historical facts in imaginative ways.

But Stone's movie is more than an exploration of responsibility for the assassination. Out of it emerges the idea that Kennedy's killing was a political coup d'état, motivated by the desire of the ruling elites to prevent him withdrawing from Vietnam, ending the Cold War and making peace with Cuba. At one point Garrison says: "We have all become Hamlets in our own country, children of a slain father-leader whose killers still possess the throne. The ghost of John Kennedy confronts us with the secret murder at the heart of the American dream." Interestingly this political thesis, a nostalgia for a world that never was, has attracted less attention than Stone's theories about the assassination.

Next page: **Movie still from *Thirteen Days*, 2000**
Directed by Roger Donaldson. Kennedy is played by Bruce Greenwood, but the human interest angle is created by focusing on Kennedy aide Kenneth O'Donnell, played by Kevin Costner.

The Kennedy dynasty is shown here in all the triumph and tragedy that seems to follow them.

Tana Hobart

Left: **Film still: *The Kennedys of Massachusetts,* 1990**
A five part television mini-series, directed by Lamont Johnson.

Next page: **Film still: *Forrest Gump,* 1994**
Tom Hanks, as Forrest, revisits milestones from the 1960s in his imaginary adventures, achieved by digital manipulation.

DAVID L. WOLPER
PRESENTA

QUEI QUATTRO GIORNI DI NOVEMBRE

This black and white documentary, so simple in its chronicling of President Kennedy's fateful trip to Dallas with his wife and the Johnsons, is absolutely devastating. The President is charming and funny and the trip is filled with local color such as residents singing Mexican music to the group—yet all the time, you know how it ends and you want to scream.

On-line film review

Left: Italian movie poster for *Four Days in November,* 1964

A documentary of Kennedy's fateful trip to Dallas, directed by Mel Stuart.

The murder of President Kennedy ... changed the course of history ... It put an abrupt end to a period of innocence and great idealism.

Oliver Stone, film director

Right: **Movie poster for *JFK*, 1991**
The movie, directed by Oliver Stone, that reopened debate about the assassination for a new generation.

Interview with Noam Chomsky

CAMBRIDGE MASS, April 2005

Noam Chomsky is professor of linguistics and philosophy at the Massachusetts Institute of Technology. He is widely credited with having revolutionized modern linguistics, and is a political and social analyst and media critic. His book *Rethinking Camelot* was published in 1993. During the years of the Kennedy Administration and subsequently, Professor Chomsky was a political activist campaigning for civil rights and against the Vietnam War.

*Your book **Rethinking Camelot**—it was published just after the release of the Oliver Stone movie …*

That wasn't my motive. My motive was that there had just been the release of a huge amount of documentary evidence. It was mostly a coincidence. In fact I barely mention the assassination.

But you mention John Newman's book, "JFK and Vietnam" …

I mention John Newman's book, yes.

And Arthur Schlesinger …

Yes, but that's all earlier.

But it was part of the background …

It was part of the background, yes. But remember what happened. In the last chapter of that book I compared the memoirists, Arthur Schlesinger, Theodore Sorensen, Roger Hilsman, and others before and after the Tet Offensive in 1968—more generally—after the war was becoming unpopular by 1967. In each case their stories were totally different afterward. For example, if you read Schlesinger's

1000 Days, which is almost a day to day account of the Kennedy Administration, there is almost nothing in it to suggest that Kennedy had a thought of withdrawing troops from Vietnam. But after the war became unpopular, in 1967–68, the stories changed—it turned out he was planning to withdraw all along, and if it hadn't been for the assassination he would have withdrawn. It's after 1967–68 that you get these stories, for instance, that Senator Mike Mansfield was pressing for an end to the war.

If you take a look at the documents, the official record, there is not a hint of it there. In fact all the later doves, including Robert Kennedy, were supporting Johnson's escalation of the war, saying that this was in the spirit of Kennedy.

In fact we now have a very rich documentary record of what happened before Kennedy's death, and you can see that in the administration spectrum he was somewhat on the hawkish side. He did reluctantly sign the proposals suggesting that the troops be withdrawn, but very conditionally, always on condition that victory has been attained, only after victory, then we can consider withdrawing troops.

That all changed after the war became unpopular, and particularly after the Tet offensive. When the business community turned against the war, when the elites turned against it, and everyone said this is costing too much, there is too much at stake, then history got rewritten. John Newman's book comes out after that, Oliver Stone comes out after that. Most of the Stone film is concerned with the assassination, not the record, though of course they interconnect because the assassination, the conspiracy claims, are based on the assumption that somebody wanted to stop Kennedy from doing the great things he was going to do. The two stories interconnect in that way.

I really wasn't interested in the assassination, I barely mention it, and as far as I can see there is not a particle of evidence that it could have been a high level conspiracy. Because policies remained the same, and not only in Vietnam, but in Cuba, in international affairs.

He was doing nothing in particular that would have led to any high level conspiracy to stop him, and the same people—his people—continued to run the programs along the lines that they were advising him and he was accepting. The people who were known later as the leading doves, such as George Ball, Mike Mansfield, Robert Kennedy, were applauding Johnson for doing the right thing, carrying out the policies of the Kennedy Administration. They had some qualms about whether they were getting in too deep, but so did everybody.

The same is true for Cuba, for instance the terrorist operations of Operation Mongoose. Kennedy stepped them up immediately after the Missile Crisis, under a different rubric. There were some moves—a move to reduce nuclear threats, nuclear agreements with the Russians—but that was under pressure from large popular movements and following the realization, which was pretty shocking, that with the Missile Crisis we came within a hair of nuclear war. I mean you have to be insane not to understand that and do something to reduce the threat, and so yes, Kennedy backtracked somewhat on the highly aggressive policies of the early years.

Whatever you think about Khrushchev, he was no fool. He knew that the Americans were trying to drive Russia into the ground by destroying the economy with an arms race. He knew that in the mid 'fifties. The Russian economy was so much smaller than the US economy, and it was surrounded by hostile enemies and so on and if they had tried to match the US in armaments they would have destroyed the economy.

Do you think that was the primary motivation for the arms race?
Well, that was Khrushchev's position, and he therefore offered Eisenhower measures to reduce armaments. The Eisenhower administration dismissed them. When Kennedy came in, Khrushchev not only made similar offers, in fact stronger ones, but even reduced offensive weaponry considerably. They didn't have intercontinental ballistic missiles, and they asked the Kennedy Administration to join in with them in cutting armaments. Kennedy thought about it, but decided to escalate instead.

So they invented this propaganda that 'The Russians are Coming' and sharply escalated military spending, including offensive military spending. Initially the Russians didn't react, but the Missile Crisis exposed the fact that they were completely vulnerable to overwhelming US power, especially after Kennedy insisted on a rather humiliating conclusion to it. Khrushchev wanted to end it with a public statement that Kennedy would withdraw the US missiles from Turkey. Russia was surrounded by offensive US nuclear missiles, right on their border in Turkey.

In fact Kennedy was surprised at the request, because he had already ordered them to be withdrawn. They were obsolete since the U.S. already had Polaris missiles in submarines. But Kennedy refused to make a public statement that he would withdraw the missiles, even though they were doing it anyway. In fact they were arming them publicly right in the middle of the crisis—a very public humiliation of Khrushchev. After the US military build-up in response to Khrushchev's steps towards de-escalation, and the exposure of Russian weakness at the missile crisis, the Russian military did initiate huge military build-up to try to match the US.

Khrushchev was right, they absolutely couldn't compete with the United States. So in the mid sixties the Russian economy starts to stagnate and you start to get all the internal problems that finally blew up in the early eighties. Maybe it would have happened anyway, there is so much complexity, you can't tell.

But the Kennedy years did have an effect, and that is when the big change took place. Whether the Kennedy people actually planned this or not is another question, but you can certainly trace it step by step, and they recognized it. If you take people like William Kaufman, a military adviser in the Pentagon, or Raymond Garthoff, what they say afterward is, we missed a big chance for a reduction of hostilities and détente back in the early 'sixties.

For the US the military budget was small relative to the total economy, and, in fact, in many ways the military spending was good for the economy. I mean, the reason why you and I use computers and the internet is that they are a spin-off from military spending. In fact military spending was the cover for socializing research and development costs for private industry. I shouldn't complain, it has paid my salary for over fifty years. That's what MIT is, it is a funnel into which the public poured money for many years under the pretext of defense, mostly Pentagon funded, and after decades came gifts which you can give to IBM, Microsoft and so forth.

This is research with lead times far too long for private capital.

And besides, it was too expensive. I mean, IBM didn't want to put the money into developing computers, but they were able to make use of the MIT and Harvard government projects to learn how to shift from punch cards to computers. So the military spending was not so much a burden on the US economy as comparable spending would be on the Russian economy. Because the US economy was at a stage where military spending could essentially fund research and development that would ultimately lead to substantial innovation and change in the economy, mostly coming out of the state sector. For the Russians that was much less true. The military spending was military. They didn't have the infrastructure, they were just a much more backward society.

Again, I do not know if this was planned, but we do know that until the early sixties Kennedy and MacMillan were very concerned about Russia, but they were concerned primarily about its economic growth. They were afraid that its economic growth was going to make it a model that the de-colonizing world would follow. In fact that's why Kennedy launched the Alliance for Progress. That was the background for the terror against Cuba.

Kennedy was afraid that the Russians would put money into Cuba and turn it into a showcase that others would try to emulate.

When the Kennedy Administration came in he had a Latin American orientation, and he had a Latin American mission, which was headed by Arthur Schlesinger, one of his close advisers, and they presented a report to the President on Latin America. Of course Cuba figured in it significantly and what Schlesinger wrote in the summary is something like this: the danger is the Castro idea of taking things into your own hands which could have a lot of appeal to others in Latin America suffering the same kind of oppression.

Out of that comes the Alliance for Progress, and of course, the other side of the Alliance for Progress, which is the iron fist. The first major military coup, there were earlier ones of course, the first major one in Latin America was Brazil, an important country, and that was initiated by the Kennedy Administration.

They tried to force Cuba to accept Russian arms. What they did was to threaten them with attack and block arms from the Western allies; and they threatened the Europeans not to send arms. No country has the right to defend itself from a US attack. Vietnam was treated the same way. Even in cases where the US is directly attacking them, they are not allowed to defend themselves.

Take Vietnam. The only moral issue remaining from the Vietnam War is, did they treat the PoWs properly? I mean, were the PoWs shot down over Iowa? They were shot down over the skies of Hanoi. They should be treated well, anyway. But is this heroic?

The truth of the matter, which we would recognize if it were any other country, was that Kennedy had invaded South Vietnam in 1962. In 1962 Kennedy ordered the US air force to bomb South Vietnamese targets, they started the chemical warfare programs, spraying crops, he started the programs to drive ultimately millions of people into strategic hamlets, which were basically concentration camps, or urban slums— that all starts in the early sixties. It didn't take place? It took place in history, but it didn't take place in recorded history.

I found out by reading the press carefully. Tucked away inside the New York Times, they mentioned that a third of the bombing missions in 1962 were being carried out by US air force planes with South Vietnamese markings. I mean, that's outright aggression, that's what you hanged people for at Nuremburg. But you couldn't get two people to talk about it, in fact to this day even the anti-war movement doesn't know about it. If you take a look at the Pentagon Papers, one of the striking things about it is that there is meticulous planning about the bombing of North Vietnam, step by step what is going to happen if we bomb there, but there was no planning about the bombing of South Vietnam, which was about triple the scale in the mid sixties.

So they just wiped it from the record …?

No. They just didn't care. The bombing of North Vietnam carried a cost. Maybe the Swedish Embassy would object if you blew them up in Hanoi, or the Russians aren't going to like it if you blow up a ship in Haiphong Harbor. Bombing the northern part of North Vietnam you are bombing the internal Chinese railroad, which happened to pass through North Vietnam where the French built it, so there is a cost to bombing North Vietnam. Bombing South Vietnam was completely costless. What are these peasants going to do if you bomb them?

So they carried out massive atrocities in South Vietnam, without any planning. There is virtually nothing in the record. In fact in Robert McNamara's memoirs, *In Retrospect*, it is very striking how he reports major decisions about bombing the South. In January 1965 he casually authorized a sharp escalation of the bombing of the South. Then a couple of weeks later he authorized a small bombing of the North. There is a huge discussion about that, but he doesn't even mention the first one, which was much more destructive.

There were people who were following it, like Bernard Fall, a leading military historian and Vietnam specialist, who was very much respected in Washington. In fact he is the only non-government authority cited in McNamara's *In Retrospect*, and it is very interesting to see what he says about it. In 1965 Fall, who was right on the ground and knew Vietnam really well, was pointing out that the bombing of North Vietnam was serious, but the bombing of South Vietnam was far worse. They were wiping out South Vietnamese society, and they may not be able to withstand it. He said it first in 1965, but said that the Vietnamese would survive and fight back. In 1967, in Fall's last book *Last Reflections on the War*—he was killed in combat—he says that by now there is a question whether Vietnam as a social and historical entity will become extinct under the attack of the most savage war machine that has ever been launched against a small country in history.

Well McNamara cites both of those comments and here's how he interprets them. In 1965 when Fall was saying you are destroying the country but in the short-run the US war is "unlosable," McNamara describes it as "encouraging news," that supported Washington's decision to escalate because "the US effort could not fail". McNamara cites Fall's 1967 statement as indicating "growing concern about the effectiveness of US military operations"—he was, very clearly, expressing grave concern about their *effectiveness*.

And that's the mentality of the Kennedy people. They sort of turned against it when it started to become too costly. If you trace the memoirs, that's exactly what you see. I went through every single one of them. I wouldn't say this unless there were a record, but there is a record. I gave a talk at the Kennedy School [of Government, Harvard University] a couple of years ago. The issue wasn't Vietnam, but Cuba came up.

I mentioned Operation Mongoose, the terrorist campaign again Cuba. Theodore Sorensen was in the audience, he was then a visiting professor at Kennedy, and when I was finished the moderator said that Sorensen would like to make a comment and was that OK. I said sure, and Sorensen got up and said that all this talk about Kennedy being involved in terrorist actions in Cuba was totally false, there was no Operation Mongoose, nothing ever happened, maybe the CIA carried out some actions somewhere we never heard about, but in the Administration we would never have permitted terrorist actions.

I tried to answer politely, but the documentary record on this is a mile high. I mean Arthur Schlesinger, who was assigned the responsibility for the terrorist war, in his biography of Robert Kennedy, says that Robert Kennedy's prime goal was, in his words, to bring "the terrors of the earth" to Cuba, and then goes on to describe some of them. But Sorensen stands up in front of a Harvard faculty club at the Kennedy School and says it never happened, and I suspect the faculty believed him. There is kind of a principle, I suspect it's a universal principle, at least I have never seen an exception, that your own crimes don't exist.

You don't know whether to laugh or to weep. This is Western Civilization. I mean, if Germany had not lost the war, how do you think they would be treating Nazism? If you lose a war, you have to accept guilt. Take the Nuremburg trials, where some of the worst criminals in history were on trial, there was no question about their guilt. Well, the trials were scandalous. I mean the basic principle was stated explicitly: they defined a "war crime" to mean a crime that you carried out and we didn't. So even bombing of civilian targets was not a war crime, because the Allies did more of it than the Germans. German criminals were able to escape sentencing if they could show that their American counterparts did the same thing. A German submarine commander escaped because he had Admiral Nimitz testify that we did those things too. So it's not that the West should be condemned, but that these aren't crimes. Can you think of one tribunal anywhere that has even dreamt of trying any of the victors?

And that's why Camelot was prettified. I mean there were some good things, but there were some monstrous atrocities, whether Vietnam, or Cuba, or the Brazilian military coup, the arms race. They practically blew up the world. We learned that in 2002, at the fortieth anniversary of the Missile Crisis. There was an amazing revelation about a Soviet nuclear submarine. We were one word away from a possible nuclear war.

I did a media search on this for the United States and there was barely a mention, and a friend did it for England, where there were two or three mentions. They needed three commanders to authorize launching a nuclear-tipped torpedo, and the third guy, Vasily Arkhipov, said no. The commanders thought they were under attack. In fact they *were* under attack, they were being attacked by US destroyers and they assumed there must be a nuclear war on, so let's release some nuclear weapons.

If that had been done there would have been retaliation with unpredictable consequences, and we might not be here. So here you are, one word away from possible nuclear war. Placing the missiles in Cuba was partly a response to US terrorist atrocities and a perceived invasion threat, we can argue how much, but that is certainly part of the reason for putting the missiles there in the first place. So here we were, just about to invade Cuba, and we learn that we were one word away from a possible terminal nuclear war, and nobody cares, just a couple of side mentions. What this tells you about the intellectual and moral culture and the priority it places on human survival, is shocking. And after the Missile Crisis was over Kennedy escalated the terrorist war again.

Why did Kennedy not ensure the Bay of Pigs invasion was a success?
At that time they were afraid, and rightly, that if they openly invaded Cuba they would just blow up the whole hemisphere. I mean if you carried out a concealed invasion it was bad enough, but if you openly invade a Latin American country, and Cuba in particular, they probably would have lost control of the hemisphere. Europe would probably be quiet and subservient, but you couldn't be sure of Latin America. I suspect, for all we know, that was their calculation, and it was probably correct. Then came the reaction: that we would carry out a terrorist war and an economic embargo, give the Latin Americans the Alliance for Progress and a lot of fancy talk, but meanwhile a heavy hand so if any other country, say Brazil, gets out of control you organize a military coup.

So Kennedy personally had to take the heat and gained a reputation for being weak and indecisive and upset the Cuban exiles …
… upset the Cuban exiles, undoubtedly …

… who were possibly involved in the assassination in one way or another.
… It's conceivable, I don't know …

… That's what certain people in Cuba believe …

Yes, that's their view. But they would want to say that. Well actually, we don't have any evidence. Frankly, I don't think the assassination issue is a very important story. I mean, if it had been a high level plot, with policy implications, then it would have been historically important. If not, then it has about as much importance as the latest murder in a downtown Boston black neighborhood. A person was killed, and that's bad. But he's not a god, just a person. If the killing of this person was not a political and historical issue, it is as if he was killed in a traffic accident. Of course it is true that in the imperial mentality that is elaborately constructed, you are supposed to mourn the passing of a god when a major figure disappears.

Do you think there is anything to the Camelot myth, civil rights …?

Kennedy did not support civil rights. He had to be dragged kicking and screaming into allowing some support for civil rights. Even after Kennedy, under Johnson, I was in the south and I remember demonstrations where demonstrators were being beaten to a pulp by the state police and fleeing to the steps of the Federal building, where Federal marshals were throwing them back into the crowd. Of course there were some exceptions, there were a couple of people in the FBI who were really trying, some people in the Kennedy Administration, but they were not really supportive, not until they were forced into it.

One time they got Martin Luther King out of jail.

At one time they got him out of jail. They did a few things which were OK, but by and large they were very resistant to the civil rights movement. Anyone who was an activist can tell you that. You were not getting support from the Federal government. There is a myth. If you go into the homes in the poor black communities in the south, you will find pictures of John F Kennedy, because an illusion has been created, that he was somehow the leader of the civil rights movement, but that happens all the time. I mean take the Reagan commemoration, which was one of the most embarrassing incidents in modern Western history; it was as if the most saintly figure in history had died. Reagan was not particularly popular as a president. But a huge PR campaign was created by the Republican Party propaganda apparatus, which is very skillful, and they turned him into a demi-god. Maybe in North Korea that kind of thing would happen, but for it to happen in a democratic society is utterly shameful.

And yes, Camelot has become that too, more for the intellectuals. I can remember here in Cambridge in the early sixties, people would fly down to Washington, fly back—these are faculty members— with their faces aglow … they had talked about Proust with Jackie Kennedy at lunch, sat next to the great man at dinner.

The one thing the Kennedy Administration understood, and they were smart, is that if you pat the intellectuals on the head and pretend you like them, they will give you a good press. And it worked.

A
Pictorial
Biography
of

JOHN
F.
KENNEDY

and his family

★ ★ ★ ★ ★ ★ ★ ★ ★ ★ ★ ★

portrayed in a card collection
of 42 historical news photos

ED-U-CARDS

Commemorating JFK

No other president, before or since, has had as many buildings, monuments or schools named after him, or is the subject of so many movies about him, his family, his wife and his assassination. The list of biographies and books dealing with aspects of his presidency is equally impressive.

Monuments to Kennedy in the United States include:

- John F. Kennedy Airport, New York—the main point of entry into the United States by air from across the Atlantic Ocean.
- John F. Kennedy School of Government, Harvard University, Boston, Mass.—a graduate school for politics and social sciences.
- John F. Kennedy Performing Arts Center, Washington, D.C.—the leading theater in the nation's political capital.
- John F. Kennedy for Research on Human Development—funded by the family in recognition of the problems of the mentally retarded such as Kennedy's sister Rosemary who spent her adult life in an institution.
- John F. Kennedy National Historical Site, Brookline, Mass.—the house where he was born and spent his early youth.
- USS John F. Kennedy CV67 aircraft carrier.

These are just a few examples—all around the world there are countless streets and other places named after Kennedy.

Left: **A box of collectors' cards**
The cards show various episodes from the President's life.

Next page: **Memorial issues**
A selection of memorial issues of magazines, including *TIME* and *Newsweek*.

LIFE

PRESIDENT
JOHN F.
KENNEDY
—
1917
1963

MEMORIAL TO GREATNESS

The Presidential Years of John F. Kennedy

$1.00

Over 100 Pages
32 Pages in
Full Color

Newsweek

DECEMBER 2, 1963 25c

JOHN
FITZGERALD
KENNEDY

1917-1963

JOHN FITZGERALD KENNEDY

"ASK NOT WHAT YOUR COUNTRY CAN DO FOR YOU . . . ASK WHAT YOU CAN DO FOR YOUR COUNTRY"

Inaugural Address Jan. 20, 1961

𝔄 Memorial Album

HIGHLIGHTS OF SPEECHES MADE BY OUR BELOVED PRESIDENT

A memorial tribute produced and broadcast by Radio Station WMCA, New York on Friday November 22, 1963. Narrated by Ed Brown; Produced by Martin Plissner and Ed Brown; Roger W. Turner, Director of News and Public Affairs. Recorded speech material from the files of Radio Press International.

2099

JFK—the gold standard

The Kennedy myth is of such potency that American politicians of all stripes try to appropriate it for themselves in the hope that some of it perhaps will rub off on them.

When the young Bill Clinton visited the White House as a member of an American Legion delegation in July 1963, he conspired to have his picture taken shaking hands with Kennedy. This photograph was used to good effect in Clinton's 1992 campaign for the presidency, in which he was portrayed as the attractive, youthful candidate with charisma and the witty repartee.

Perhaps the most memorable attempt to don Kennedy's mantle was during the 1988 presidential campaign. Dan Quayle, a forty-one-year-old Republican senator running for the vice presidency, met Lloyd Bentsen, the Democratic candidate, in a nationally televised debate. Quayle, countering charges of youth and inexperience, made the claim: "I have as much experience in the Congress as Jack Kennedy did when he sought the presidency." Bentsen countered with one of the most famous retorts in the history of American political debate: "Senator, I served with Jack Kennedy. I knew Jack Kennedy. Jack Kennedy was a friend of mine. Senator, you're no Jack Kennedy."

Previous page: **Long Playing record cover**
Memorial album featuring highlights from John F. Kennedy's speeches.

Right: **Bill Clinton shakes hands with Kennedy, July 26, 1963**
The young future president was visiting the White House from Arkansas as a member of an American Legion delegation.

A portrait is first and foremost a painting. The subject is secondary.

Aaron Shikler

Previous page: **U.S. artist Robert Rauschenberg, December 1967**
With a 1964 pop art silkscreen painting featuring Kennedy.

Left: **Posthumous portrait by Aaron Shikler, 1970**
The painting now hangs in the White House.

It is our intention and hope to make a gift of this home to the American people so that future generations will be able to visit it and see how people lived in 1917 and thus get a better appreciation of the history of this wonderful country.

Rose Kennedy

Right: **John F. Kennedy National Historic Site**
83 Beals Street, Brookline, Mass.,where the Kennedy family lived from 1914–20, and where four of the nine children were born.

Next page: **Sixth Floor Museum, Dealey Plaza, Dallas**
The museum is located in the Texas Schoolbook Depository, from which the Warren Report concluded that Lee Harvey Oswald fired the shots that killed Kennedy.

Not one single member of the
Solomon Islands resistance ever
turned in an American soldier.

Eroni Kumana, one of the Solomon Islanders
who rescued Kennedy

The eternal flame

The decision to bury Kennedy in Arlington National Cemetery rather than his home city of Boston was Jackie's, and it was she who chose the site, with Robert McNamara's help. She wanted a shrine close to the nation's capital, where her husband would be remembered as a national hero. She was perfectly sure of what her decision meant in the context of American history.

He belongs to the people.

Jackie Kennedy

Only one other U.S. president was buried at Arlington—William Howard Taft, who died in 1930. (Woodrow Wilson, who was buried at the National Cathedral in Washington, D.C., was the only other president to be buried outside his native state.)

Kennedy's first visit to Arlington was on Armistice Day, November 11, 1961, to place a wreath at the Tomb of the Unknowns. He returned for the 1963 Armistice Day commemoration, eleven days before his assassination.

He was honored with the grandest funeral ever seen for a U.S. president. An eternal flame was lit by his widow. Jackie took the idea from the flame that has burned at the Tomb of the Unknown Warrior to commemorate those that died in World War I, at the Arc de Triomphe in Paris.

Previous page: **The John F. Kennedy Library and Museum, Boston, Mass.** The museum was designed by I. M. Pei, and opened in 1979.

Jackie had a great sense of the dramatic. There were no wrong notes.

Janet Auchincloss, Jackie Kennedy's mother

Right: **Arlington National Cemetery, Virginia, March 16, 1967**
Jackie Kennedy places flowers on her husband's grave, at the ceremony following the reburial of his body in a permanent grave site.

Above: **Arlington National Cemetery, Virginia, November 22, 2004**

The eternal flame burning on the 40th anniversary of Kennedy's death.

Jacqueline Kennedy ... lit a flame that is to burn forever on his grave—against the day that anyone might forget that her husband had been a President ...

Mary McGrory

Photo Credits

Ollie Atkins, © George Mason University Libraries, Fairfax, VA
pages 67, 107, 136, 144, 157.

The Associated Press/EMPICS
pages 36, 51, 406–407.

CORBIS
© **Corbis:** page 166–167; © **Bettmann/Corbis:** pages 42, 110–111, 121, 179, 215, 236–237, 244, 332; **Larry Downing/Reuters/Corbis:** page 414; © **Dave G. Houser/Corbis:** page 408–409; © **Jeffrey Markowitz/Corbis Sygma:** page 367.

Getty Images
pages 81, 260, 322–323, 328; **AFP/Getty Images:** pages 40–41, 240–241; **Consolidated News Photos/Getty Images:** page 399; **Time Life Pictures/Getty Images:** pages 2, 87, 103, 105, 114–115, 116–119, 126, 122–123, 135, 138, 146–147, 158, 161, 171, 177, 185 (© Sanford Kossin/Life Magazine,) 227, 288, 312–313, 331, 400–401.

John Fitzgerald Kennedy Library, Boston, MA
pages 10–11, 17, 18, 27, 32–33, 35, 45, 46, 49, 55, 56, 62, 68–69, 70, 73, 76, 80–81, 84, 88–89, 95, 98–99, 129, 154–155, 162–163 (© Newsweek Inc.)**,** 199, 232-233; **John F. Kennedy Library Foundation:** pages 14, 39, 65; **Robert Knudsen, White House/John Fitzgerald Kennedy Library:** pages 204, 263, 269, 277; **Abbie Rowe, National Park Service/John Fitzgerald Kennedy Library:** pages 5, 254–255, 259; **Cecil Stoughton, White House/John Fitzgerald Kennedy Library:** pages 186, 188–189, 194, 202–203, 207, 212–213, 224, 235, 264, 270, 274, 284, 293, 294–295, 297, 319; **Cecil Stoughton, U.S. Signal Corps/John Fitzgerald Kennedy Library:** page 413; **Turgeon Studios/John Fitzgerald Kennedy Library:** page 59.

National Park Service
Courtesy **John F. Kennedy National Historic Site, Brookline, Mass.,** pages 20–21, 405.

Quotation Credits

CHAPTER 1

p15 Nigel Hamilton, *JFK: Reckless Youth*, p48 (hereafter referred to as Hamilton)

p16 Hamilton, p649

p22 Gore Vidal, *Palimpsest, A Memoir*, p19 (hereafter referred to as Vidal)

p24 Richard D. Mahoney, *Sons & Brothers*, p27

p29 Hamilton, p149

p38 Hugh Sidey, Introduction to *Prelude to Leadership: the post-war diary of John F. Kennedy*, pxxiv

p43 *Boston Globe*, interview with Joseph P. Kennedy, November 10, 1940

p50 Hamilton, p268

p57 Hamilton, P404

CHAPTER 2

p85 Blair, Joan and Clay, Jr., *The Search for JFK*, p87 (hereafter referred to as Blair)

p86 Blair, p356

p90 Hamilton, p787

p104 *www.brainyquote.com*

p106 *www.brainyquote.com*

p109 C. David Heymann, *A Woman Named Jackie*, p121 (hereafter referred to as Heymann)

p112 Sarah Bradford, *America's Queen* p87 (hereafter referred to as Bradford)

p118 John F. Kennedy, *Profiles in Courage*, p19

p127 Heymann, p265

p139 Hugh Sidey, *Remembering Jack*

p141 *Haverhill Gazette*, October 5, 1952

CHAPTER 3

p159 Sally Bedell Smith, *Grace and Power*, p8

p160 Bradford, p191

p168 John F. Kennedy, *Inaugural Speech*, January 20, 1961

p172 *St Louis Globe Democrat*, January 15, 1961

p176 John F. Kennedy, *Inaugural Speech*, January 20, 1961

p182 Joan Meyers (ed.), *John Fitzgerald Kennedy...as we remember him*, p182 (hereafter referred to as Meyers)

p195 Telephone call to Alan Shepard minutes after he returned to Earth, May 5, 1961, *www.bbc.co.uk*

p197 Robert Dallek, *John F. Kennedy, an Unfinished Life*, p400 (hereafter referred to as Dallek)

p200 *International Herald Tribune*, February 6, 1989, cited in Carlos Lechuga, *Cuba and the Missile Crisis*, p39 (hereafter referred to as Lechuga)

p208 Tripartite Conference on the Missile Crisis, Havana, Cuba, January 10, 1992, cited in Lechuga, p25

p208 Ernest R. May and Philip D. Zelikow (eds), *The Kennedy Tapes: inside the White House during the Missile Crisis*, p41

p215 *www.historychannel.com/speeches/archive*

p225 *Address to the Latin American Diplomatic Corps*, the White House, March 13, 1961

p231 John F. Kennedy, *Speech in West Berlin*, June 26, 1963

p243 Homer Bigart, *New York Times*, February 25, 1962

p245 John F. Kennedy interview with Walter Cronkite on CBS television, September 2, 1963

p258 Martin Luther King Jr., *Speech to the March on Washington for Jobs and Freedom*, August 28, 1963

p261 John F. Kennedy, *Statement on the March on Washington for Jobs and Freedom*, August 28, 1963

p265 John F. Kennedy, *Remarks prepared for delivery at Dallas Trade Mart Luncheon*, November 22, 1963

p267 Thomas W. Benson, *Speechwriting, Speechmaking, and the Press*

p276 Meyers, p207

p281 Charlotte Mosley (ed.), *Love from Nancy: The Letters of Nancy Mitford*, p460

p281 Vidal, p311

p286 *LOOK* magazine, January 2, 1962

p287 Seymour Hersh, *The Dark Side of Camelot*, p104

CHAPTER 4

p292 William Manchester, *The Death of a President*, p121

p296 Anthony Summers, *The Kennedy Conspiracy*, p307 (hereafter referred to as Summers)

p300 Summers, p197

p329 Alistair Cooke, Letter from America, BBC, November 24, 1963

p333 Summers, p311

CHAPTER 5

p365 Charles E. Schwarz, *Lonely Detective and Other Mysteries*

p378 *Washington Post*, June 2, 1991

p412 Sally Bedell Smith, *Grace and Power*, p444

Bibliography

There are many biographies of Kennedy, and a large literature dealing with various aspects of his political career and presidency. I list below some of the books in the English language that particularly helped me to develop my own point of view about Kennedy.

There is, of course, a bias. I was a young schoolboy in England and just becoming aware of politics at around the time Kennedy was president. The Cuban Missile Crisis was virtually incomprehensible to me at that time, and it was not until years later that I began to understand a little of what was behind it. When Kennedy was assassinated a year later my main reaction was one of puzzlement that such an event could happen.

Many years later I developed a deep interest in Cuba. I have visited the island many times and written about its political economy and culture. The more I learned about the early years of the Cuban Revolution, the more I realized that the predominant myth of Kennedy as a liberal figure championing a New Frontier and the independence of colonized nations did not hold water. I discovered that the Kennedy administration had been responsible for a relentless secret war against Cuba, and that this war was intimately linked with the Missile Crisis that had so puzzled me as a young boy. As I dug further I came to realize that Kennedy's obsession with Cuba was part of his general approach to the Cold War. It was not a question of whether Kennedy was a good man or a bad man, and indeed there is every indication that he could be charming, engaging, and fun to be with. But the point, I came to believe, was that Kennedy was a fully paid up member of the elite of the most powerful nation in the world, and that this elite had a very clear plan as to how it intended to maintain its position—through wielding enormous economic and military power around the globe. Kennedy would never have got close to becoming president if he were not a firm supporter of that plan.

So that is my bias. It is my firm conviction, however, that if the true history of U.S. relations with Cuba, Vietnam and with the Soviet Union were more widely known, and if the civil rights movement were better understood, then many more people would share my viewpoint. I offer the following selective reading list for those who would like to take their understanding further.

Two important accounts appeared in 1965: the standard, semi-official account of the presidency, *A Thousand Days: John F. Kennedy in the White House*, by Arthur M. Schlesinger, Jr., a member of the administration; and an account by Kennedy's main speech writer, Theodore C. Sorensen, *Kennedy*. Kennedy's Press Secretary Pierre Salinger wrote an engaging account from his perspective in 1966, *With Kennedy*.

The best biography dealing with Kennedy's childhood and youth is Nigel Hamilton's *JFK: Reckless Youth* (1992), which draws on extensive original interviews with family and friends. Unfortunately the promised second volume never appeared. Laurence Leamer's *The Kennedy Men* (2001) and Robert Dallek's *John F. Kennedy: an Unfinished Life* (2003) cover Kennedy's whole life in considerable detail. Geoffrey Perret's *Jack, A Life Like No Other* (2001) is another interesting account.

Noam Chomsky's *Rethinking Camelot: JFK, the Vietnam War and U.S. Political Culture* (1993) is a very careful analysis of the escalation of military intervention in Vietnam under Kennedy. Seymour Hersh, in *The Dark Side of Camelot* (1997), provides much new information on Kennedy's personal life and his foreign adventures, particularly his obsession with Castro's Cuba. *Palimpsest* (1995)—the memoir by Jackie Kennedy's step-brother-in-law, Gore Vidal—offers fascinating glimpses of Kennedy and the creation of what he calls the "National Security State" that support Hersh's approach. Fabián Escalante, the former head of Cuban Intelligence who I interviewed for this book, is the author of *The Cuba Project: CIA Covert Operations 1959-62* (2004) and *Operation Mongoose* (2004) both of which provide detailed accounts of Kennedy's secret war against Cuba.

Among the growing literature which disagrees with Chomsky, Hersh *et al*, suggesting that Kennedy really intended to wash his hands of Vietnam, and pull the troops out whatever the cost, are Arthur Schlesinger Jr.'s biography *Robert Kennedy and His Times* (1978); John M. Newman's *JFK and Vietnam* (1992); Robert S. McNamara's *In Retrospect: the Tragedy and Lessons of Vietnam* (1995); and Gareth Porter's *Perils of Dominance: Imbalance of Power and the Road to War in Vietnam* (2005).

Since the collapse of the Soviet Union much new information has emerged regarding the Missile Crisis, spurred by a series of conferences involving key participants from Cuba, Russia, and the United States. Carlos Lechuga's *Cuba and the Missile Crisis* (2001) is a fascinating account of that dangerous episode, and is particularly interesting as it is told from the Cuban side. Aleksandr Fursenko and Timothy Naftali provide an extraordinary account based on declassified Soviet and U.S. documents in their *"One Hell of a Gamble": Khrushchev, Castro, Kennedy and the Cuban Missile Crisis 1958–1964* (1997). The tapes of the White House discussions during the crisis have been made available in Ernest R. May and Philip D. Zelikow (eds), *The Kennedy Tapes: inside the White House during the Cuban Missile Crisis* (1997). The National Security Archive at George Washington University continues to unearth documents of great importance to the study of U.S. policy during the Cold War

Howard Zinn provides a subtle yet succinct introduction to the civil rights movement in his *A People's History of the United States* (1980), with a guide to further reading.

An excellent overview of Kennedy's foreign policy is offered in Thomas G. Paterson (ed.)'s *Kennedy's Quest for Victory: American Foreign Policy, 1961–1963* (1989). Christopher Simpson's *The Splendid Blond Beast: Money, Law and Genocide in the Twentieth Century* (1995) provides an acute analysis of U.S. policy towards Hitler's Germany which is helpful in understanding Joseph Kennedy's political stance and the milieu in which his son originally learned his politics. Noam Chomsky has written extensively about the origins of American Cold War policy and the relationship between its foreign and domestic aspects, for example in *Deterring Democracy* (1991).

Books on Kennedy's assassination are legion. One of the best accounts that challenge the Warren Commission Report is Anthony Summers' *The Kennedy Conspiracy* (1998, updated). Jim Marrs provides an extensive step-by-step overview of assassination theories in *Crossfire: the plot that killed Kennedy* (1989). An interesting collection of press articles generated by the controversy following the release of Oliver Stone's movie *JFK* may be found in Oliver Stone and Zachary Sklar's *JFK: the Book of the Film* (1992), which also contains the screenplay. Fabián Escalante's *1963: the Plots to Kill Kennedy and Fidel Castro* (2005) provides detailed information from Cuban Intelligence about Cuban émigré links with Lee Harvey Oswald, Jack Ruby and Mafia figures with links to the CIA.

Acknowledgments

I wish to thank Ambassador Carlos Lechuga, General Fabián Escalante and Dr. Noam Chomsky for agreeing to be interviewed for this book. Each in their different ways helped me to focus my thoughts more steadily, though none of them is responsible for any errors of fact or interpretation in what I have written.

The staff of Ocean Press are to be congratulated for the many books they have published regarding Cuba and the Cold War, including the books by Carlos Lechuga and Fabián Escalante listed in my bibliography. I thank them for helping to arrange the interview with Fabián Escalante.

Special thanks to my wife, and publisher, Zaro Weil, who challenged my views throughout and contributed greatly to my understanding of the Kennedy presidency. My thanks also to my editor, Yvonne Deutch, who has an extraordinary gift for engaging with a text and its author which may only be described as Celtic.

Index

Page numbers in *italics*
refer to illustrations

First published by MQ Publications Ltd
12 The Ivories
6–8 Northampton Street
London, N1 2HY
Tel: 020 7359 2244
Fax: 020 7359 1616
email: mail@mqpublications.com
website: www.mqpublications.com

North American Office:
49 West 24th Street, 8th Floor
New York, NY 10010
email: information@mqpublicationsus.com

MQP Handbooks Director: Gareth Jenkins
MQP Handbooks Series Editor: Yvonne Deutch

ISBN: 1-84072-676-8

10 9 8 7 6 5 4 3 2 1

Printed in China

71431

★ 1957

Feb — The Senate "Rackets Committee" on labor union corruption begins hearings with JFK as a Democratic member and Robert F. Kennedy as chief counsel

Jul 2 — JFK calls for the independence of Algeria from France

Nov 27 — Birth of Caroline Bouvier Kennedy

★ 1958

Nov 4 — JFK reelected to the Senate with a massive majority

★ 1959

Jan 1 — Fidel Castro ousts President Batista and Cuba's nationalist revolution triumphs

★ 1960

Apr 5 — JFK wins the Wisconsin Democratic primary election for the presidency

May 11 — JFK wins the West Virginia primary election

Mar 17 — President Eisenhower approves CIA operation against Cuba

Mid-Jul — CIA organizes private meeting for JFK with four Cuban émigrés to inform him of plans to depose Fidel Castro

Jul 13 — JFK receives the Democratic nomination for president

Sep 12 — JFK tells Protestant ministers in Houston that his Catholic faith is of no consequence to his presidential ambitions

Sep 26 — JFK's first of four televised debates with Vice President Richard M. Nixon

Nov 8 — In the closest popular vote in American history, Senator Kennedy defeats Richard M. Nixon to become the 35th president of the United States

Nov 25 — Birth of John F. Kennedy Jr.

★ 1961

Jan 20 — JFK is sworn in as president on a freezing day, the youngest elected president and the first Roman Catholic president. His brother, Robert F. Kennedy, will be his attorney general

Mar 1 — JFK signs an executive order creating the Peace Corps

Apr 17 — The Bay of Pigs invasion of Cuba by Cuban émigrés, illegally backed by the U.S. government, fails and JFK takes the blame

May — JFK's first state visit to Canada

Jun 3-4 — JFK meets Soviet Premier Nikita Khrushchev in Vienna

Aug 13 — The Berlin Wall is erected, closing off East Germany from West Berlin

May — Freedom Riders attempt to racially integrate interstate buses in Montgomery, Alabama

Dec — Bobby takes control of Operation Mongoose, a multi-agency plan to undermine Castro's Cuba run by Brig. Gen. Edward G. Lansdale

Dec 19 — Joe Sr. paralyzed by a stroke

★ 1963

Feb 27 — FBI Director J. Edgar Hoover warns Kennedy aide Kenneth O'Donnell and Bobby that JFK is having an affair with mobster's moll Judith Campbell (Exner)

Solomon Islands by a Japanese destroyer; he wins the Navy and Marine Corps Medal in helping to rescue his crew. John Hersey's article "Survival" about JFK and PT 109 appears in the *New Yorker,* June 1944

★ 1944

May 31 — JFK enters the U.S. Naval Hospital in Chelsea, Massachusetts with back injuries

Aug 12 — Joe Jr. dies in an exploding plane over England and is posthumously awarded the Naval Cross

Sep 10 — William Hartington, British husband of JFK's sister Kathleen, is killed in action in Belgium

★ 1945

Apr-Jul — JFK works as a reporter for Hearst newspapers. He covers the San Francisco conference drawing up a charter for the United Nations, and the British parliamentary elections

★ 1946

Nov 5 — JFK is elected as U.S. representative for the 11th Boston Congressional District

★ 1947

Oct — On a visit to London JFK is diagnosed as having Addison's disease

★ 1948

May 13 — JFK's sister Kathleen and her lover die in a plane crash in southern France

Nov 2 — JFK is reelected to Congress

★

Nov 7 — **1950**
JFK is again reelected to Congress

★ 1951

Jan — JFK visits France, Italy, Yugoslavia, Germany and Spain for a month

Oct — JFK visits France, Iran, Israel, Pakistan, India, Vietnam and Japan with his brother Bobby and sister Pat

★ 1952

Nov 4 — JFK challenges Sen. Henry Cabot Lodge Jr. for the U.S. Senate seat of Massachusetts and wins by 70,000 votes

★ 1953

Jan 14 — Robert Kennedy appointed assistant counsel to the Senate Subcommittee on Investigations (the McCarthy Committee)

Sep 12 — JFK, 36, marries Jacqueline Bouvier, 24, at Newport, Rhode Island

★ 1954

Oct 21 — JFK nearly dies as a result of a back operation

Dec 2 — JFK is one of two senators absent from the Senate vote censuring Sen. Joseph P. McCarthy

★ 1955

Feb 11 — JFK again almost dies during a second back operation. During his recovery, he writes *Profiles in Courage*, which wins a Pulitzer Prize for biography in 1957

★ 1956

Aug 17 — JFK fails to win the Democratic Vice Presidential nomination, but leaves the convention as his party's rising star

Aug 23 — Jackie gives birth prematurely to a stillborn daughter while JFK is cruising in the Mediterranean

the
John F. Kennedy
handbook